GREEK ISLAND DELIGHTS

THOMSON HOLIDAY COLOUR EDITION IN WHERE TO GO IN GREECE SERIES

GW00504684

SETTLE PRESS
HIPPOCRENE BOOKS INC.

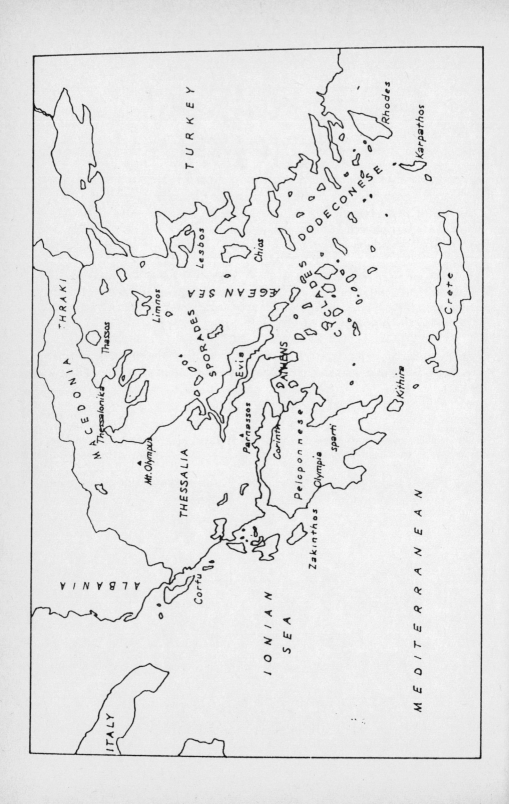

Foreword

We are delighted to be associated with another of Trevor Webster's guides to the Greek Islands. The popularity of our Greek Island brochure, "Simply Greece", has shown that interest in Greece as a holiday destination has never been greater and has highlighted the need for a practical, yet readable, guide to the islands.

This latest in the successful "Where to go in Greece" series has been written in the highly-personal style of someone who knows and loves this unique country. It covers twelve of the most popular islands stretching like a string of pearls around the Greek mainland.

Whether you are a committed Grecophile or a first-timer, we are sure you will find this book invaluable in helping to plan and enjoy your next holiday in Greece.

Thomson Holidays

While every reasonable care has been taken by the
author and publisher in presenting the information in
this book, no responsibility can be taken by them or
by Thomson Holidays for any inaccuracies.

© 1990 Trevor Webster
First published by Settle Press (Wigmore)
10 Boyne Terrace Mews
London W11 3LR

ISBN (Hardback) 0 907070 60 4
         (Paperback) 0 907070 61 2

British Library Cataloguing in Publication Data
Greek Islands delights. – (Where to go in)
   1. Greece. Islands Visitors guides
   I. Series
      914.95'0476

Published in United States by
Hippocrene Books Inc
171 Madison Avenue,
New York N.Y. 10016

ISBN 0-87052-598-0

Printed by Villiers Publications Ltd
26a Shepherds Hill, London N6 5AH

Contents

1. The Greek Islands

Greek islands are pure magic. They have an air of warmth, continuity and great age. And they give an immediate sense of belonging and having a stake in all you survey.

Each one is unique. If you ever find an island that reminds you of another, they are sure to be at opposite ends of the Aegean or Adriatic. The next one across the water always offers a complete contrast to the one you are on.

It is impossible to answer the question which is the best. Or which one has the best beaches. Or, even which is your favourite. It is equally hard to say which is the best chain or group. Their variety and our personal taste rule out easy ranking. How do you allow for the way some islands appeal on early visits to Greece, then pall on better acquaintance, while the appeal of others grows stronger?

There are around 3,000 Greek islands in all, but the majority are only small barren rocks. About 170 islands are inhabited and, of those, about 100 are accessible and worth visiting for the normal holiday pursuits of eating, sleeping, resting, walking, swimming and sight-seeing.

Among the major tourist islands, some like Mykonos, Kos, Samos and Paros have proved versatile in absorbing and changing their nature and communications without losing their heads.

A few islands are in danger of being over-run and turned into foreign colonies with discotheques, international bars and sprawling campsites along the beaches. They appeal to many young people, but do not have the same ethnic, get-away-from-it-all atmosphere of other islands.

Santorini, Corfu, Crete and Kephalonia stand out in any group for spectacular scenery, competing with Rhodes and Samos with their surviving wonders of the ancient world.

The Cyclades are almost all burnt brown islands, with the Meltemmi wind adding its force to the hot sun in the summer months. The north Aegean isles, Ionian isles and those close to Turkey are greener. For those who find the summer heat oppressive, the coolest and greenest islands of all are the most northern, including Thassos, Corfu, Skiathos and Kefalonia.

Almost every island in Greece has a sandy beach, or beaches, somewhere around its coastline. These are usually on the rough side where the waves pound the shore and have shattered the pebbles over thousands of years. Equally, most islands have serviceable shingle, pebble and rock beaches on the opposite calmer shores.

Sandy beaches have more eye appeal, are usually softer to lie on, and are ideal for families with children. But, shingle, pebble and rock beaches have their virtues too. They are much better for snorkelling, since fish are more attracted by rocks and weed than by smooth flat sand. They can be cleaner, too. Sand beaches more often play host to globules of tar washed up from ships, producing indelible stains on body and clothes.

In the wake of its more developed Mediterranean neighbours such as Italy, Spain and Portugal, and with some faltering steps, Greece is developing into an activity holiday country. Where big hotels have sprouted up on Rhodes, Corfu and Crete, tennis courts, riding schools, golf courses and other organised sports, have all followed.

Water-skiing and windsurfing have grown up in similar places and have expanded in recent years to most tourist isles large and small. Greek waters are ideal for both learning and practising windsurfing and water-skiing, being tideless and usually warm and wave-free. With these activities, you are dependent on the people renting the equipment. They are usually in evidence during the summer since they want to maximise the return on their equipment, but they are scarce in spring, autumn or winter, because many are foreigners who return home out of season.

Nudism is officially banned everywhere in Greece and can attract a stiff legal penalty. Most islands now sport notices on their quaysides warning about the law. Yet the police have turned a blind eye to let topless and nudist beaches flourish on a few islands like Mykonos, Paros, Rhodes and Corfu, where the beaches are mainly populated by tourists. And, if you find a beach to yourself well away from any local eyes there is nothing to prevent you stripping off discreetly for a swim or to let the sun in on pale areas.

Snorkelling in Greece is a delight, thanks to warm, clear waters. There are parts of the world with more or bigger fish, but there is something about the underwater scene in Greece that appeals – where it is not sullied by too many plastic bags, rusty ironwork and broken fishing lines.

Greek islands are the stuff that dreams are made of. And picture postcards too. Whether they are brown or green, they are usually framed in a bright blue sky and sea. They feature white wedding cake churches, brightly-painted villages, yellow beaches and multi-coloured flowers.

Donkeys, goats and lizards are still more common sights than buses, takeaways or TV sets.

The twelve islands covered in this book are all beautiful, and boast a rich variety of beach and sight-seeing delights. For that reason they rank among the main tourist islands of Greece, and their most popular resorts will be crowded in the summer.

But all are big enough to offer quieter spots. Even in mid-summer you should be able to find a path or a beach or a restaurant to yourself, if that's what you are seeking.

The Greek islands are hot, cheap and friendly. Indeed Greece is the hottest country in Europe with the southern isles on the same meridian as north Africa. Most areas record 300 days of sunshine a year.

It is also one of the cheapest countries in Europe, challenged only by Portugal and Turkey this side of the Iron

Curtain. Although prices rise 20 or 30 per cent a year, the Greek drachma has been devaluing itself at an even greater rate.

You can find a double room in a modest hotel for £5–10 a night, buy dinner for two for £5–10, and take a bus ride for 10–20p and a modest taxi ride for £2. A bottle of beer costs around 60p, a coffee 30p and a bottle of wine in a restaurant runs from 60p to £2.

The islands remain friendly in spite of the march of tourism and a get-rich quick mentality spreading on a few of them. It has not smothered the natural exuberance of the small beach taverna, or the welcoming smile of the donkey-borne peasant.

2. Recommendations

Families — Corfu, Zakynthos, Rhodes, Kos, Paros, Crete, Skiathos

Golfers — Corfu, Rhodes

Tennis-players — Corfu, Kefalonia, Rhodes, Crete

Windsurfers — Corfu, Rhodes, Kos, Paros, Crete, Mykonos, Skiathos, Thassos

Motorists — Corfu, Kefalonia, Rhodes, Crete

Motor cyclists — Corfu, Kefalonia, Kos, Paros, Santorini, Samos, Thassos

Cyclists — Zakynthos, Kos, Paros, Samos, Thassos

Walkers — Crete, Skiathos, Samos

Campers — Corfu, Rhodes, Kos, Crete, Paros, Thassos

Back-packers — Corfu, Rhodes, Crete, Paros, Thassos

Naturalists — Corfu, Kefalonia, Zakynthos, Rhodes, Santorini, Crete

Painters — Corfu, Zakynthos, Rhodes, Mykonos, Paros, Santorini

Wine Buffs — Kefalonia, Zakynthos, Rhodes, Kos, Santorini, Paros, Samos

Culture Vultures (Classical) — Rhodes, Kos, Crete, Santorini, Samos

Culture Vultures (Byzantine) — Rhodes, Kos, Crete

Students — Corfu, Rhodes, Crete, Thassos

Teeny-Boppers — Corfu, Kos, Paros, Thassos

Ravers — Corfu, Kos, Mykonos, Paros, Crete, Thassos

Nudists — Corfu, Rhodes, Mykonos, Crete, Skiathos

Hermits — Crete

Gays — Mykonos

Beach Bums — Corfu, Zakynthos, Rhodes, Kos, Crete, Paros, Mykonos, Skiathos, Thassos

Trend-setters — Zakynthos, Skiathos, Samos, Thassos

Plutocrats — Corfu, Zakynthos, Rhodes, Mykonos, Santorini, Skiathos

Honeymooners — Corfu, Zakynthos, Rhodes, Skiathos, Samos

Island-hoppers — Corfu, Kefalonia, Paros, Mykonos, Kos, Skiathos

Seasoned travellers — Samos, Santorini, Kefalonia, Zakynthos

Solitaries — Crete

Gourmets — Corfu, Rhodes, Paros

The rest of us — Zakynthos, Paros, Rhodes, Samos, Thassos

Webster's Rating Tables

	Direct Flights	Beaches	Watersports	Sites	Scenery	Eating	Webster rating (out of 10)
Corfu	✓	★★★★	✓	★	★★★★	★★★★	8
Crete	✓	★★★	✓	★★★©	★★★★	★★★	8
Rhodes	✓	★★★★	✓	★★★★	★★★★	★★★★	9
Kos	✓	★★★	✓	★★★	★★★	★★★	8
Skiathos	✓	★★★★	✓	★★	★★★	★★★	8
Kefalonia	✓	★★★	✓	★©	★★★★	★★★	8
Zakynthos	✓	★★★★	✓	★©	★★★★	★★★	8
Mykonos	✓	★★★★	✓		★★	★★★	8
Paros		★★★★	✓	★	★★★	★★★★	9
Santorini	✓	★★★	✓	★★★△	★★★★	★★★	8
Samos	✓	★★★	✓	★★	★★★★	★★★	8
Thassos		★★★★	✓.	★★	★★	★★★	8

© Caves   △ Volcano

3. The Olive Isle – Corfu

Corfu or Kerkira is not only one of the most beautiful islands in Greece, it is one of the most beautiful in the world, ranking with the best of the Caribbean and the South Seas and outshining most of the other jewels of the Mediterranean.

It is a rich tapestry of green mountains, wooded hillsides, white villages and sandy beaches interwoven with the reds, yellows and blues of wild flowers and blossoms, and framed in the blue of the Ionian Sea. A Garden of Eden in modern Greece.

Corfu is an olive isle. Its dominant colour is olive green in light and dark shades, which are worn by herbs, shrubs and cypress trees after a winter's rain and a summer's sun. It is the greenest island in Greece.

Then there are the olives themselves. Every Greek island has olive trees, but none so many as Corfu. The Venetians, who occupied the island for four centuries, planted over a million of them and they have multiplied like the tribes of Israel.

You can see them everywhere on the island today, lining the roads and hillsides in serried groves. Whole families of gnarled and wizened old grandfather and grandmother trees surrounded by the mature fantastic shapes of their sons and daughters and their young straight, thrusting offspring. At the last count there were over 4 million on the island.

Corfu is one of the most northern isles in Greece and also the most westerly, apart from three of its own small satellite isles, which helps to explain its lush fertility, and its cosmopolitan nature.

Thanks to frequent showers of rain in the winter months it escapes the extremes of heat and dryness that burn many Greek islands bare and brown. It has always enjoyed an enormous number of visitors from Western Europe, who have found it easily accessible thanks to its position at the base of the Adriatic, directly across the Ionian Sea from the heel of Italy and Sicily, which was a vibrant part of the Greek world in ancient times.

Most visitors have come as conquerors – the Corinthians, the Romans, the Sicilians, the Venetians, the French, the Italians, the Germans and even the British, who were the only occupying power to quit voluntarily. Yet all of these races find a warm welcome on the island today, in the best traditions of the ancient people who welcomed Odysseus when he was washed ashore on his long voyage from Troy 32 centuries ago.

Corfu is the most popular holiday island in Greece, taking no less than a quarter of British package tourists. But it is big enough to absorb tourists without losing its true nature. And it has something for everyone.

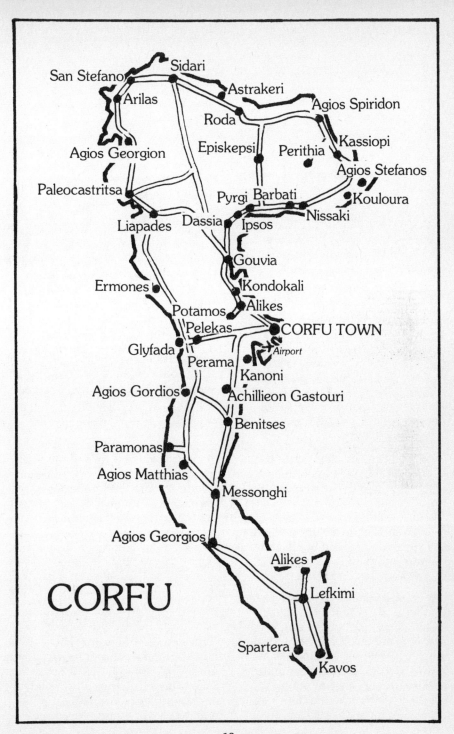

CORFU

Its most popular east coast resorts like Benitses, Ipsos, Gouvia, Dassia, Kanoni, Perama, Kavos, Messongi, Moraitika and Kontokali have been transformed in recent years by the development of villas, hotels, restaurants and discotheques to match the swelling crowds of summer tourists. Kassiopi, Rhoda and Sidari on the north coast and Paleocastritsa on the west coast are also fast-developing into multi-purpose tourist meccas.

If you want all the modern delights of a package holiday in the Med like wind-surfing, water-skiing, beach beds, a range of shops, restaurants serving English dishes, bars with cocktails and music, and a choice of discotheques, these are the places to aim for.

If you are yearning for peace and quiet, uncrowded beaches, and a refuge from motor-boats and piped music, try west coast resorts like Arillas, Agios Stefanos, Agios Georgiou (in the north and often called Agios Georgeous), Glyfada, Agios Gordis, Agios Georgios (in the south) and San Barbara.

Often you can find a stretch of beach to yourself alongside or close to a resort with all the trimmings. Kavos has been expanding like crazy in recent years and now has 80 bars, most of them with music, but it also has two miles of sandy beach and you can quickly walk to an uncrowded seashore or unspoiled countryside.

It is always possible to get away from it all on Corfu. The interior of the island remains proud and unspoiled. The villages have barely been touched by tourism and the local people are friendly. And you can always find a healthy strip of beach to yourself somewhere on the island. Often a whole beach out of season.

Visit in May or October, when the weather is hot and sunny by the standards of English summers, and you may wonder that the island ever gets crowded. Wild flowers and magnificent sunsets are more noticeable than busy beaches or discotheques.

Corfu has a character and a culture that differs from all other Greek islands and has a curious British flavour that has not stemmed from the tourist flood of the past twenty years.

You can buy ginger beer along with Greek lemonade and resinated wine from the cafés flanking the main square in Corfu town and occasionally watch an afternoon cricket match where loud cheers are reserved for any batsman hitting a six into the crowded tables clustered beneath the arches of the town's fashionable Liston arcade. But by 8 p.m. in the evening the same square will be thronged with courting couples and Greek families with babies in prams indulging in the traditional Greek volta – an evening out walking the town.

Many Corfiots speak good English, especially in the town and the popular tourist resorts, and every schoolchild seems to learn 'Hello' and 'Goodbye' as soon as they have learned to walk. Two bars around the harbour area are called Dirty Dick's and the Spoty Dog. But if you mingle with local men in cafés where they sit sipping coffee and playing backgammon, you will hear animated conversation in Greek, which is often concerned with weather, fishing or local politics.

You will soon notice that half the men on the island are called Spiro after the island's patron saint, Saint Spiridon, who is paraded around the island four times a year on feast days and can also be viewed in his coffin in the church of the same name that towers over Corfu town.

Apart from the brief occupation in the 19th century, Corfu has many connections with Britain. It is renowned as the birthplace of the Duke of Edinburgh and was for years a favourite haunt of the Durrell family, which writers Lawrence and Gerald have celebrated in several books.

It is sometimes said that the island is 'not really Greek', usually by people who haven't visited much of the country, and it may have something to do with Corfu's lush green garb, which makes it look more like Capri or Majorca than the bare, burned Aegean islands. It looks as though it is rained on every other day. In fact, it rarely rains during the peak holiday months from May to October.

Corfu has the ambition to stay top of the pops on the British holiday market and will do so, thanks to its pleasant climate, beautiful landscape, friendly people and cheap prices stemming from a continuous devaluation of the Greek drachma in recent years.

The island has miraculously avoided the overdevelopment and the high-rise ghettos that scar slabs of the Spanish coastline and Sicily. You have only to walk 100 yards inland from any of the coast resorts to see a black-clad granny riding a donkey laden with firewood crossing herself as she passes a wayside shrine. You can walk along any harbourside and see fishermen drying their nets or beating a squid on the rocks to tenderise it for cooking. The old lives on alongside the new.

Long and narrow for most of its length with a wider head in the north, Corfu looks like a giant seahorse from the air. For a third of its length, the island faces Albania, and the gap between the two narrows to about 1½ miles in the north. The high shore in the north-east affords visitors a glimpse of that mysterious Communist country, which is still living in the 1940's and behind the Bamboo Curtain, even though the Chinese have long since lowered it on their country and let Capitalism rush in.

From Corfu, it looks as though there is nobody stirring in Albania, but yachtsmen, fishermen and windsurfers who stray across the channel into Albanian waters are often intercepted by gunboats and detained for 24 hours. Corfiots living in the north of the island sometimes tune in to TV programmes from Albania and also Yugoslavia and Italy, complaining that reception from mother Greece is difficult.

Ease of access from Western Europe, along with its natural beauty and friendliness, earns Corfu around 500,000 visitors a year, far more than any other Greek island, and two-thirds of them come from Britain. Tourism is rising at a rate of around 15 per cent a year and 100,000 people are now passing through Corfu Airport in a peak month like July. So it is hardly surprising that there are pressure points.

Although the British built some good roads by Greek island standards in the 19th century, some have too many potholes and narrow corners for today's tourist traffic. The airport terminal, at the head of Kanoni lagoon airstrip, which seemed such a dramatic improvement when it replaced a tiny shed in the 1970's, now bulges at the seams when two or three planes are landing or taking off around the same time.

However, there are plans to double

15

the airport's capacity over a three-year period. More parking space is being built for aeroplanes, more check-in areas, a new bar and restaurant and even more toilets, according to the plans.

Beaches

You can swim almost anywhere around the coast of Corfu, so you will never be far from a beach. But the beaches along the calmer east coast facing the mainland, which is popular with British holidaymakers, tend to be white shingle and pebble, with the odd strip of sand, while those along the surfy west coast facing the Ionian Sea are all of the yellow sand variety that dreams are made of. So are those on the north coast.

One guide to the island says that there are 6½ outstanding beaches on Corfu, but if you spend long enough there, you will be able to count up to ten times that number, and still have the three northern satellite islands of Mathraki, Othoni and Erikoussa to spare. The beaches are mostly easy to get to too, thanks to coastal roads running along the north and east coasts of the island and good signposting along the wilder west coast.

Corfu town has no beach worthy of the name and you swim at your peril off the long promenade around Garitsa Bay, which receives the effluent from some of the town's big hotels. It's safer to walk to Mon Repos beach at the southern end of town or to one of the strips just off Kanoni, close to the airport, but better still to travel 10–20 kilometres north or south of the town if you want to swim on the east coast.

South of the town lies the villa coast of Perama and Benitses, where there are dozens of small swimmable shingley coves – and a number of big hotels have sprung up. To the north lie the major resorts of Kontokali, Dassia, Gouvia and Ipsos, boasting long beaches where pebble gives way to sand and you can find every kind of beach sport from windsurfing to paragliding. Nissaki also has the beach sports, but is more pebbly.

Gouvia's beach is almost always calm, whatever the weather, because it is sheltered by a big and almost enclosed bay. It is an unusual limpid scene with an old church on a sandspit contrasting strangely with all the water sports available on the beach.

If you go further north, to the coast that juts out towards Albania, as if it is trying to touch it, you are in Durrell country – the setting of Lawrence Durrell's 'Prospero's Cell' and Gerald Durrell's 'My Family and Other Animals'. There lie a succession of coves containing fishing hamlets and sheltered pebbly beaches under names like Koloura, Kalami, Kentrona and Agios Stefanos until you reach Kassiopi on the north-east tip, which has become a popular resort and gives the best view over to moody Albania. It has no great beaches, but there are pretty swimmable coves to rest off the revels of the night before, soak up the sun and cool off with the odd dip.

South of Benitses, there are more swimmable coves around Miramare, Moraitika and Messonghi, but the best beach on the whole east coast is the long stretch of sand at Kavos in the deep south. Kavos has grown into a major resort with hotels, restaurants and villas, and is visited by boats from higher up the coast, attracted by its long sandy beach, which stretches away towards the southern tip.

16

There is no need to travel so far, though, if you are staying in Corfu town or one of the east coast resorts close to it. The west coast abounds in beautiful strands and four of the most famous, Glyfada, Agios Gordis, Ermones and Myrtiotissa, are all within easy reach of the town.

In fact, Glyfada and Agios Gordis are growing into sizeable resorts on their own account, thanks to good roads, a string of restaurants and villas and a handful of big hotels that have opened in the past ten years. Glyfada, only 17 kilometres from Corfu town via the colourful village of Pelekas, and Agios Gordis, a slightly longer drive through some stunning coastal scenery, are both good family resorts with shallow waters and deep sand, and can be crowded in high season, but both are surrounded by cliffs and steep wooded slopes that helps to give a feeling of isolation.

Ermones is not such an impressive beach as the others, but it is a famous one. It is believed to be the bay where a ship-wrecked Odysseus was washed up and discovered by Nausicaa and her handmaidens on his long voyage from Troy. It has another claim to fame nowadays because it is the nearest beach to Corfu's Golf Club, a miniature Garden of Eden stretching down the Ropa Valley.

If you rise early enough, you can do 18 holes before lunch and swim in the afternoon in a bay where history, or at least mythology, was made. Though many golfers buy a week's golfing package, including transport, from Glyfada and might prefer that beach for relaxed swimming off perfect sand rather than Ermones.

Myrtiotissa has a different claim to fame. It is a narrow beach beneath a tiny whitewashed monastery and steep cliffs with big rocks rising from the sand. Remoteness from the road and bus stop long since suggested it as a nudist beach. Scandalised local peasants have regularly complained to the police and fines have been levied, but in between times the police turn a blind eye and the nudity lives on.

If you want to go topless on the west coast of Corfu, there are plenty of suitable places. Like the vast sands of Agios Georgios, which stretches down the south-west from the Korission Lagoon and the sand dunes lying on the seaside of Korission. This area now boasts half a dozen simple restaurants. A bus stops near a signposted side-road and you can drive a car or scooter closer to the beach, but beware of getting stuck in the sand.

It is the biggest and best beach on the island. The stretch by the lagoon is backed by sand dunes and the rest by high cliffs. There are now four access roads and two emerging resorts at Agios Georgios and San Barbara (or Marathia Beach) with a sprinkling of rooms to stay in. Even in mid-summer you can escape other tourists on this long beach, but there are no trees to shade the hot sun.

It has not developed as quickly as a beach of the same name, Agios Georgios Bay in the north-west, a superb curve of fine sand which was free of all habitation in the late sixties, and reached only down a third class riverbed road via the village of Pagi. It now has a string of restaurants and a tarmac road, but is still long enough to absorb crowds of day trippers coming around by boat from Palaeocastritsa and allow you many yards of beach to yourself.

There are many other shorter sand beaches in the west. Paliokastritsa, the biggest resort on this coast, has its own quota of sandy bays, though they do become crowded with residents of the resort's many hotels. You can find less crowded beaches at Paramonas, reached through the 'black forest' of Agios Mattheos, Kontogialos immediately south of Glyfada reached by a short walk downhill from the village of Pelekas, and at a handful of small fishing villages now opening up as resorts in the north-west, Afionas, Arillas and Agios Stefanos.

Arillas has the best beach, a long thin stretch of sand. It also has caique trips to the deserted islet of Diaplo and a half hour walk across the cliffs brings you another beach in the neighbouring, but quite different, little resort of Agios Stefanos.

Paramonas makes a great day out if you have a car or scooter. It has a restaurant, an inn with a few rooms and a lovely sandy beach, which never seems to get crowded.

The north coast has the traditional resort of Sidari, which has strange sandstone rocks rising out of the sea clustering around one with a hole in it called the 'Canal D'Amour'. It is a haunt for lovers where a wish can come true and visitors often wade through the canal in hope and good faith.

Roda, also on the north coast, has grown into a resort from the small fishing village that has always been there, thanks to its long sandy bay that also encompasses the village of Anharavi. It is ideal for families, because the sea is so shallow and calm.

A third sandy stretch can be found on the north coast at Agios Spiridon, a small village off the main coast road which has a chapel in honour of the island's patron saint and also has a good beach for children. It makes a pleasant walk from Kassiopi.

There are also good beaches on the three small islets an hour by boat from Sidari. Erikoussa has dazzling sand beaches on two of its three sides.

What the east coast lacks in sand, it makes up in an exotic underwater seascape for snorkelling and spear-fishing, but most of the sand beaches of the west and north coasts are framed in clusters of rocks, which offer exciting sea life. Most of the big resorts, like Ipsos, Dassia, Gouvia, Perama, Benitses, Kavos, Paleocastritsa, Agios Georgios and Roda offer windsurfing and water-skiing and some have scuba-diving. Dassia and Ipsos have paragliding.

You can hire yachts in Corfu town and rent a boat from a local fisherman almost anywhere by negotiation, whether you want to go fishing or just see what kind of beach lies around the next headland.

You can play golf on some of the greenest greens in Europe at Corfu's 18-hole course in the Ropa Valley close to Glyfada and Ermones. You can also take lessons and hire all the gear.

Corfu town has a tennis club, but few courts.

The best places to find tennis courts are in big hotels like the Roda Beach, the Corcyra Beach, the Kerkira Golf – which is on the opposite side of the island from the golf course and only 2 miles north of Corfu town – the Park at Gouvia, the Chandris at Dassia, the Dassia Beach, the Messonghi Beach and the Regency at Benitses. Many of the big hotels also offer riding.

18

Nightlife

Nightlife is not so formal or organised in Greece as in Western Europe, but almost everyone from old men to courting couples and families with babies in prams get involved in it. Usually outdoors and in a theatrical way that shows off the extrovert side of the Greeks.

If you scratch a Greek, he will open a bar or a restaurant and there are thousands on Corfu. Most of them have dozens of tables pouring out on to a pavement, a square or a harbourside, and they surge to life by night as people gather to drink beer, ouzo or coffee, to share a groaning table covered with tiny dishes, or in the case of ladies on their own to feast on sticky cakes.

Those who can find tables in the most popular spots such as the main square in Corfu town or the harboursides of the coastal resorts are then treated to a display of walking known as the volta. There are no fixed rules and no age and time limits. People walk up and down for hours seeking gentle exercise, showing off their new clothes, and stopping for an occasional chat with friends or to take a drink at one of the cafés on the side.

Wining and dining out is so cheap and full of fun that nightlife for most tourists is an evening in an outdoor restaurant preceded or followed by drinks in a bar. You can sample Greek specialities such as souvlakia on sticks, Greek salads topped with onions and cheese and fish served with lemon, accompanied by local Corfu wines, or retsina, the cheap golden wine of the country laced with pine essence and often served in baby (50 centalitre) bottles.

In high summer many of the outdoor restaurants on Corfu, especially in the coastal resorts, have music to dine by, traditional Greek tunes mingled with slightly tarnished juke box melodies, and it is not unusual to see local people or even waiters start an impromptu syrtaki or group dance, which can involve every diner in the restaurant in time.

If you fail to come across this scene by yourself and want an evening of Greek dancing, you should always be able to find a tour going off one evening from any of the big hotels to a taverna specialising in Greek dancing and dining for an all-in price.

One place where you are certain to find it is 'The Village' – a place you mustn't leave Corfu without visiting, according to hundreds of signs along the roads. For an entry fee, which might include a drink, you can look over a recreated Greek village with handicraft shops and tavernas. The tavernas offer local delicacies, wine and Greek dancing often for an all-in price. Although it seems odd to create an artificial village on an island teeming with pretty villages, a visit to The Village can make an enjoyable evening out.

If you are staying outside Corfu town, is also makes sense to go into town for a night and eat at one of the old-established restaurants around the square such as the Aegli or the Averof where they serve a mixture of Greek and Italian dishes and a few Corfiot specialities which are not found everywhere in Greece such as sofrito and gouvetsi.

The Old Fort in Corfu town has sound and light performances and there are a number of open-air cinemas, which offer a mixture of old Hollywood hits and obscure Italian westerns with Greek subtitles and Greek comedies with elusive slapstick humour. Every so often the lights come on for a round of coca cola and snacks.

The most formal nightlife in Corfu is at the Casino a few kilometres uphill from the airport near the village of Gastouri, which can be reached by local bus or taxi. James Bond tried his luck at the table in 'For Your Eyes Only' and so can you so long as you are properly dressed (gentlemen with jackets and ties) and can pay the price of the entry ticket and your stake money.

The casino is set in the Achilleion Palace, built in an unusual mixture of styles by the sad Empress Elizabeth of Austria, which is often described as ugly, but for my money is the most beautiful casino in Greece. It stands proud and tall in a superb setting of formal gardens, surrounded by cypress trees, high in the hills with magic views of Corfu town way below.

If you don't fancy your luck at the tables, stroll down to the semi-circular restaurant a hundred yards down the road to eat in a romantic setting and watch the twinkling lights of Corfu and ships crossing the Ionian sea.

Another magic place to eat at night for good food and one of the world's great views is at the Belvedere Restaurant halfway up the winding zig-zag road leading to the Troumpeta Pass. Again you can see the bright lights of Corfu town and the coast resorts winking far below.

Greek discotheques wax and wane with the seasons and more often than not are housed in rough outdoor premises which would be unsuitable for winter use. There are exceptions in Corfu town and around the hotels in the big coastal resorts. Benitses, Gouvia, Ipsos, Dassia, Messonghi and Kanoni are resorts that have a couple of discos each which all swing to the early hours through summer. Gouvia even has an underground disco, which is a rarity in Greece.

Not to be missed: On Corfu

Corfu town ranks with Rhodes as the two most stylish towns in Greece, and both owe a lot to the Italians. Corfu's tall buildings, narrow alleys and peeling grandeur are reminiscent of Venice without the canals. The two forts have Venetian origins, and the main square or Esplanade with its pigeons and house martins has connotations with St Mark's Square.

It is a delightful town to stroll round, soaking up atmosphere, especially the bustling port, the grand sweep of Garitsa Bay and the Esplanade (or Spianada) with its Liston arcade – so called in the days of British occupation because only people on the list of top families were allowed there. Pause at the Church of Saint Spyridon and look at the gold and silver votive offerings to the island's patron, and also at the 12th century church of Saints Jason and Sosipater.

Otherwise, it is not a great town for sights, other than the town itself. They are of the 'worth doing on a dull day' category. The two fortresses, or their remains, call for imagination rather than great staying power but they do give good panoramic views of the town. The Palace of Saint Michael and Saint George, which originally housed the British High Commissioner and later the Greek royal family, has a small museum housing, of all things, an Asian art collection.

There is an archaeological museum in the town along the promenade of Garitsa Bay, just down from the

Tourist Office, which is modern and airy and has two big finds, a Gorgon pediment from a Temple of Artemis dating back to the fifth century BC and an ancient lion of the same era. But the museum does not stand comparison with its rivals in Athens, Thessalonika or Crete. There is also the town cathedral, Mitropolis, which houses the headless remains of Saint Theodora, who arrived on the island with Saint Spyridon. But the real delights of Corfu are outside the town, reached either by bus from the station next to the New Fortress, by hired car, bicycle or scooter. Car-hire, alas, is one thing that costs a lot more in Greece than in Britain – upwards of £20 a day – but may be worthwhile for a family for a day or two to do a quick tour of the island and mark down places to return to at leisure.

Scooters and bicycles can be hired in numerous shops towards the seafront of the old town, as well as in many beach resorts, and provide a much cheaper alternative, but it is worth making sure before you quit the town that scooters are powerful enough to carry two people uphill and then take real care on unmade roads. You see too many tourists on Corfu with bandages around bloody ankles and Greek medical treatment is not so good that it is worth risking a road accident.

Immediately south of Corfu town – and reachable by bicycle – lie the island's most famous sights. First, Mon Repos, the villa where Prince Philip was born, then Mouse Island and the Achilleion Palace.

Mouse Island, or Pontikonissi, with its 13th century chapel, and its twin islet of Vlacherna, lie in Kanoni Bay and are almost a trade-mark of Corfu, much photographed by visitors and

much seen on postcards. This idyllic scene lies only a few yards from the lagoon runway of Corfu airport, so the scene is also a familiar one to travellers arriving and departing by jet from colder climes.

The Achilleion lies a few kilometres beyond that and is easily the grandest building on Corfu. Many art experts have described the palace and the statues in its gardens as ugly, grotesque or misconceived, but their setting amid green hills, trees and gardens makes them one of the most beautiful sights on this and any other Greek island. Ignore the experts and enjoy the palace, the gardens and the statue of the dying Achilles, wounded in his heel, but still holding his warrior's spear. Spare a thought for the sad Empress Elizabeth who built this grand place and was assassinated by a crazy fanatic in Geneva.

Below the palace on the coast lies the Kaiser's Bridge, the remains of an old harbour built by the second owner of the palace, and it is worth exploring beyond there to the southern tip of the island. The old fishing village of Benitses has been transformed into a swinging resort, but bears no resemblance whatever to Palma, Majorca, and the road down to Kavos at the southern tip of the island passes through some delightful countryside and inland villages. In the south, the Korission lagoon is worth visiting and Kavos is another fishing village that has been turned into a thriving resort, with regular boats from Corfu town, the mainland and the island of Paxos to the south of Corfu.

While in the south, linger a little in Lefkimmi. It is a big, honest town with graceful mansions and a canal-like river stretching down to the sea. Pretty cafés are now springing up along its banks. It is a painter's delight and a strange contrast with the fleshpots of Kavos a few miles down the coast.

The coast north of Corfu town is even more developed with beach resorts such as Kondokali, Gouvia, Dassia and Ipsos, but is also a delightful tour as far as Kassiopi, pausing to visit the bays of Koloura and Agios Stefanos where the Durrells lived and to take a close look at Albania. The best view is probably from Kassiopi, where visitors can also look over traces of a Hellenistic town visited by Nero and a Byzantine fortress.

The most spectacular roads for high exotic scenery and pretty villages are those to the beach resorts of the west coast. Pelekas, with the Kaiser's Seat, where he used to watch the sunset, is a short trip and a rewarding one, while Paleocastritsa with its hills, sandy bays and 13th century castle is a delightful excursion. For the best view of the resort and its six bays, ascend the road that winds up from Paleocastritsa towards Makrades.

Even more spectacular is the high road over the Troumpeta Pass to Sidari and Roda. Pause at the little café at the summit for a coffee and the view.

That journey is strictly for car, scooter or bus, but there are many invigorating walks inland to pretty hill villages from the coastal resorts. Energetic climbers can tackle Mount Pantocrator, and a good alternative for the not-quite-so-energetic is a walk uphill to an abandoned hill village on the north slope of Pantocrator called Perithia.

It is reached by road inland from Kassiopi and Loutses, which is tarmaced for most of its way. When the tarmac runs out you have a stiff uphill walk for two hours or a 15-minute drive for a glimpse of what village life on Corfu was like 200 or 300 years ago. Most of the inhabitants have moved down to the coast and the place is now inhabited by only two families, but they do serve drinks from a tiny bar, which are most welcome after the climb.

Perithia makes an odd contrast with Kassiopi a few miles away, where the tavernas rock nightly to loud canned music and visitors sunbathe topless in adjoining bays.

Worth visiting: Off Corfu

If you fancy spending two or three days on one of the other big Ionian islands, Kefalonia or Zakynthos, you can island-hop in a light plane, which makes the trip in an amazingly short time.

Although the northern part of Corfu faces Albania, and it is not possible to travel across the Straits to that mysterious country, there are plenty of fascinating places to visit from Corfu. You can go north by boat from Sidari or sometimes Kassiopi to the three tiny satellite isles of Othoni, Erikoussa and Mathraki, south from Corfu town to the island of Paxos or east from the port by ferry to the mainland of Western Greece at Igoumenitsa.

The three northern islands are about an hour away by boat and seem more remote. Othoni has a medieval castle and a bay called Calypso where it is thought Odysseus might have stayed with the nymph of the same name on the voyage from Troy. All three are cute little isles and undeveloped, though a small two-storey hotel has recently been built on Erikoussa and there are two tavernas, so it is a comfortable place to stay to enjoy the good sandy beaches, which are almost continuous stretches on two sides of the island and hardly crowded.

Paxos is a jewel of an island, a good deal smaller than Corfu, but much bigger than the three northern islands, which takes about three hours by ship from Corfu town, but about half the time by boat from Kavos on the southern tip of Corfu. Boats also ply between Kavos and Parga.

Parga is the main seaside resort of Western Greece. Set between the towering hills of Epirus, it has three fine sandy beaches on separate bays with tiny islands offshore, and resembles an island port more than a mainland resort. Tourism has brought windsurfing, discotheques and regular boat trips to Corfu and Paxos, but just outside the town you are in wild countryside.

Epirus is a land of mountains, lakes and rivers with giant tortoises, birds of prey, occasional snakes and storks, which live on the steeples of churches in every town. It also boasts good roads, so it makes a good day's outing from Corfu by ferry with hired car or scooter.

If you want to see something grander than the seaside resort of Parga, drive inland to Dodoni, site of the oldest oracle and the best amphitheatre in Greece. It is a magnificent green glade, surrounded by high mountains, and the nearby restaurant offers much better fare than is usually found in such places serving archaeological sites.

If you drive east 100 kilometres, you will reach the main city of Western Greece, Ioannina, which is a bustling place set off a lake with a big part in Greek history of the past few centuries. It was the seat of the Turkish Governor and the castle promontory of Ali Pasha still dominates the lake.

There is a restaurant on the island and dozens more along the shore of the lake, where they serve frogs' legs, trout and eels from the lake. Zitza wine makes a good complement to this unusual Greek freshwater fare.

Just south of Parga off the main road to Preveza lies another of the great sights of Epirus, the Necromanteion. The mythical entrance to the underworld, the site of the Oracle of the Dead and Persephone's Grove visited by Odysseus in the Odyssey, it now comprises a few ruined buildings and an underground chamber. It makes up in eerie atmosphere what it lacks in size, enough to inspire regular day trips from Parga and Paxos.

If you lack time or don't fancy hiring a car or scooter, it is still worth taking the ferry crossing from Corfu to the mainland port of Igoumenitsa for the day. Igoumenitsa is a major ferry link with both Italy and Corfu and as much a harbour as a town, but it has good honest eating at restaurants along the quay and a respectable beach curving around the bay.

If you are staying on Corfu for a fortnight and want to see more of the mainland and its sights, it is not difficult to drive or take a bus beyond Ionnina to the monastery wonderland of Meteora, to drive down to Delphi on the north coast of the Gulf of Corinth, or even to visit some of the sites of the Peloponnese. But plan a two-day trip with overnight stay to make the journey comfortable.

23

4. Zorba's Isle – Crete

Crete is easily the biggest island in Greece and the second most popular destination for British holidaymakers after Corfu. They are attracted by its popular beach resorts, wild mountainous landscape, moody atmosphere, and Minoan past; a past like the Minotaur, which shares its name, that is part history and part myth.

The 'Big Island' gave birth to Europe's first known civilisation, ruling the Eastern Mediterranean from grand palaces at Knossos, Phaistos and Malia with colourful frescoes, modern drainage and a mysterious bull and axe cult. But there is no historical evidence for the dreadful Minotaur, a half-man, half-bull monster which enjoyed an annual diet of young men and women from faraway colonies like Athens. Nor are there any traces of the legendary King Minos, who started the dynasty, beyond the name.

There are modern myths and half-truths about Crete too. It is often described as the most Greek of Greek islands, blessed with picturesque towns, surrounded by superb beaches and wild scenery.

It is no more Greek than Paros, Naxos or Santorini – or, for that matter, Corfu, which is sometimes said to be 'unGreek' – and in fact joined the nation later than all of them.

The island's capital, Heraklion, is the ugliest town in the Aegean, but its three other main towns, Chania, Rethymnon and Agios Nikolaos, are stunning. Much of the coastline is rocky, so that you sometimes have to travel miles for a good beach, but there are many long sandy stretches on all four shores.

Crete has wild scenery, but is not as wild as it sounds. It is heavily populated with big towns and high-rise hotels along the north coast and more intensively cultivated inland. Its fertile valleys and plains, fed by rivers that run down from Mount Ida, the White Mountains and Mount Dikti, supply 90% of the Greek currant crop, a quarter of its olive oil, an eighth of its wine and a big slice of its tobacco. It has acres of ugly plastic greenhouses on the west and south coasts.

What is beyond dispute is that Crete has a unique history and character. And it is so big that it offers a great variety of places and scenery.

It has a good network of modern roads along all four coasts, including a motorway along the well-developed and windy north coast, where the Cretan Sea crashes on yellow sand, and along the south coast where the Libyan Sea is calmer, the sand is sometimes grey and the climate is warmer the year round thanks to the balmy breezes that drift across from Africa. It is also criss-crossed from north to south by good link roads that run down mountain passes and steep,

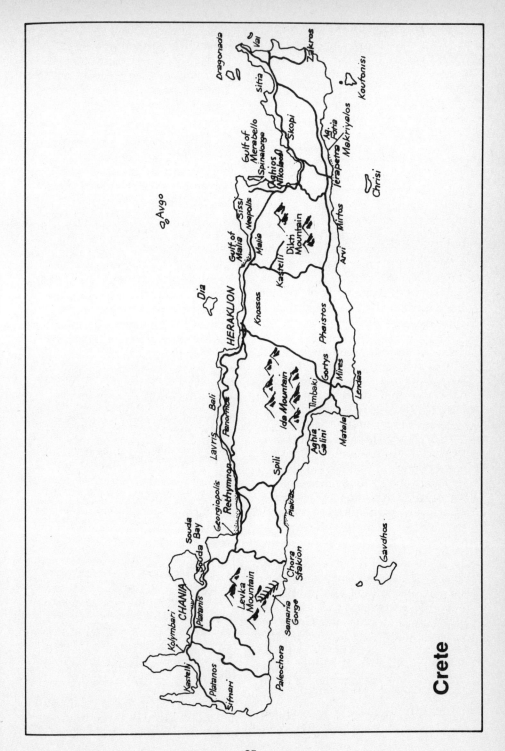

Crete

narrow gorges where the sky and valleys are squeezed between high mountains and the villages are often prettier than on the coast.

These mountains and ravines have witnessed many battles, right up to the Second World War when Crete was the focus of the German invasion of Greece. Cretan mountain men and shepherds can look wild and woolly in their traditional dress with long leather boots, headbands, drooping moustaches and long curved knives stuck in baggy trousers. Village weddings can be colourful affairs with both men and women in national dress performing the cyclical syrtos and the romantic sousta with endless drinking to the music of the lyre, mandolin and bagpipes (or tsabouna).

Crete is the land of the lotus-eaters and Zorba the Greek. It was the setting for the TV series, 'Who pays the Ferryman?', which helped kindle interest in the island in Britain. It has given birth to many famous sons, including the statesman, Eleftherios Venezelos – who shares his Christian name ('Freedom') with many other Cretans – and El Greco the painter whose great colourful religious works grace many art galleries in Spain and a room or two in London's National Gallery.

More than any other Greek island, it seems self-sufficient and able to support itself without tourism. But tourist development is well-established in Eastern Crete along the 'Cretan Riviera' in the nomos (or district) of Heraklion and that of Lassithi or Agios Nikolaos, while it is catching up fast in Western Crete in the nomos of Chania and that of Rethymnon.

Visitors who want to get away from it all should head away from the four big towns, especially Heraklion – after seeing Knossos and its beautiful archaeological museum – and head either inland or for the west and south coasts. As a general rule, Western Crete is less touristy than Eastern Crete.

Crete has two airports at Heraklion and Chania, both served by international flights as well as internal flights from Athens, Rhodes, Santorini and Mykonos.

The island is also well-served by big ferries, which call at no less than five ports on the north coast – Heraklion, Souda (for Chania) Kastelli, Rethymnon, Agios Nikolaos and Sitia. They connect Crete with Piraeus, Rhodes, Karpathos, Santorini and the southern Peloponnese via Antikithera. It is also a frequent port of call for cruise ships.

Crete is easy to travel once you are there, so long as you can face long distances. It has a good road network linking all main centres and good bus services radiating out from Heraklion. Car hire is available in all main towns and so are scooters, mopeds and bicycles.

As the southernmost Greek island, it has the longest summers and the mildest winters. You can tan in hot sunshine until the end of October and swim in the Libyan Sea without undue pain in December and January, though the mountains attract more rain throughout the year than you might see on Rhodes, which is a fair way north of Crete, and the meltemmi wind blows harder across Crete in July and August than it does on Rhodes.

Crete is where mythology and history met around 1500 BC. The meeting place was the labyrinth of Knossos, known in legend as the lair of the dreaded Minotaur.

In mythology the Minotaur was the offspring of a bull sent by Poseidon and Pasifae, the wife of King Minos. It was slain by Theseus. The myth was put to rest by Sir Arthur Evans, the British archaeologist, who excavated Knossos around the turn of the century. His findings suggest that the Minoans did rule the known world from a labyrinthine palace at Knossos, and did exact tribute from colonies like Athens. Indeed young Athenians were trained as acrobats to take part in dangerous bull dances, which are now portrayed on frescoes at Knossos.

No island can more rightly claim to be the cradle of European civilisation. When the Minoans ruled Crete – and probably Santorini and the Eastern Mediterranean 3,000 to 4,000 years ago, they lived in richly-frescoed palaces with modern drainage and lavish entertainment. Their women wore make-up, jewellery and fashionable clothes, bared their breasts, plaited their hair and carried long jugs decorated with sophisticated patterns.

Knossos, the most famous Minoan site built around 1700 BC stands as a proud memorial to that period and that civilisation. It also shows signs, along with other Minoan palaces at Malia, Phaistos, Zakros and Agia Triada, of having suddenly been overwhelmed by a great natural disaster around 1500 BC. It was almost certainly the eruption of the volcano on nearby Santorini and the tidal wave that followed that gave rise to the legend of the lost city of Atlantis and started the Biblical flood which launched Noah's Ark.

There are other legends and myths about Crete. It was said to be the birthplace of Zeus, the father of the Gods, who was borne by Rhea, the wife of Cronus, and hidden in a cave on Mount Dikti. The cave still makes a pleasant walk from the village of Psychro, providing one more link between myth and history.

In the historic period that started around 1500 BC, Crete was invaded by the Myceneans, the Romans, the Venetians and the Turks. The Myceneans left linear B script, which was also found at Mycenae. The Romans left the remains of a handsome capital and a code of laws carved in stone, at Gortys south of Heraklion and a short way east of Phaistos. The Venetians left beautiful harbours at Chania, Heraklion and Rethymnon and promoted the Cretan School of Artists. The Turks built houses with wooden balconies around the harbours and left the memory of a bloody invasion from 1645 to 1669.

The Turks held Crete longer than most of their Aegean possessions and it only became part of Greece in 1913 after a long campaign by the island's best known statesman, Eleftherios Venezelos. Twenty-eight years later, in 1941, it was occupied again, this time by the Germans, when it became the focus of the Nazi invasion of Greece.

If was the site of the sea-borne Battle of Crete and a major retreat by British forces through the southern port of Chora Sfakion, which is marked by a memorial plaque on the harbour wall. It was also famous for the Cretan Resistance Movement, which was joined by a handful of British soldiers and stayed active in the mountains until the end of World War Two.

Eastern Crete

Eastern Crete contains the nomos (or

district) of Heraklion, fanning out from the island capital of the same name, and that of Lassithi, which surrounds Agios Nikolaos, for years the main holiday centre of the island. The coast between the two towns is the main holiday coast of Crete and is often called the 'Cretan Riviera'.

It boasts a string of popular resorts like Agia Pelagia, Hersonisos, Sissi, Malia and Elouda opposite the islet of Spinalonga. They have all grown up over the past 20 years and now rival Agios Nikolaos for tourist developments, such as hotels, restaurants, discotheques and water sports. On this strip you get a fair quota of high-rise and crowds with your sandy beach.

East of Agios Nikolaos is a wilder region served by the Cretan ring road as far as Sitia, an honest but dull little town. The south coast, which is also served by the ring road, is a good deal quieter with Ierapetra and Matala its only major resorts.

The two nomoi also contain the six major Minoan sites on Crete – Knossos, Phaistos, Malia, Zakros, Gournia and Agia Triada, plus the fascinating Roman capital of Gortys and the pretty hill village of Kritsa. Which go a long way towards explaining why tourism flourished first at this end of the island.

They also abut Mount Dikti, with the cave where Zeus was reputedly born, and the Plain of Lassithi, famed for its thousands of tall windmills. Mount Ida forms a pivot for the whole of the island, dividing the nomos of Heraklion from that of Rethymnon and Eastern Crete from Western Crete.

Beaches on Eastern Crete

The most dazzling beaches in eastern Crete are on the east coast at Vai and the south coast at Makriyalos, but there are several adequate stretches of sand on both sides of Heraklion and along the 'Cretan Riviera', which stretches east from the capital as far as Malia. There are windsurfers for hire and other watersports at all these resorts.

You can find a narrow sand beach around the long bay to west of Heraklion and at Agia Pelagia on the next promontory. The only snags are the view of rusting ships and oil refineries around the bay and a slight feeling of claustrophobia at Agia Pelagia where a narrow strip of sand is sandwiched between a big package tour hotel complex and a series of bars and restaurants. East of Heraklion most people make for Amnissos just beyond the airport, which is a pay beach and tends to be crowded, but is good sand and is an easy bus ride from a stop by Heraklion harbour.

Like the Athenian Riviera, the Cretan Riviera becomes more scenic the further you travel along it. Another beach stretches from Chani Kokkini all the way along to Creta Camping or Gournes with a wilder look than Amnissos, but not such good sand. There are good sand beaches at Hersonissos and Stalis, though both are flanked by bustling promenades or bars, restaurants and discotheques.

Malia has an even longer stretch of sand, with dunes at one end and half a dozen good restaurants, but it can get crowded. You can escape the crowds at Sissi, at the eastern end of the bay of Malia, though you have to walk 15 minutes from the harbour to find a series of three remote little sandy coves.

The main road turns inland after Malia and hits the coast again at Agios Nikolaos, which despite its reputation as a holiday centre has no beach of its own, other than three tiny imported strips of sand by the big beach hotels. There are, however, a number of cove beaches around the Gulf of Mirabello at Istro, Kalo Horio and Pachia Ammos south of Agios Nikolaos and 10 kilometres north at Elounda where there is a good stretch of sand opposite the islet of Spinalonga with all the watersports and a good selection of restaurants.

Sitia has a long shingle beach, which stretches along the bay as far as Agia Fotia, but it is somehow a dull one. More exciting for those with transport is palm-fringed Vai just across the tip of eastern Crete's last spidery peninsula. It has superb sand, a good restaurant and a small island to swim out to and snorkel around. It looks divine at dawn and dusk. The only snags between those times are the crowds, who somehow find their way to this apparently remote place.

The east coast is barren and rocky, but it does have a pretty pebble beach at Kato Zakro east of the Minoan site flanked by a number of good simple rooms and tavernas.

My accolade for the best all-round beach in eastern Crete would have to go to Makriyalos 25 kilometres east of Ierapetra where the main road south from Sitia hits the Libyan Sea. Ierapetra ('Holyrock') itself is a dull town, although it has a pretty promenade, a passable beach, and qualifies as the biggest town on the south coast of Crete, but Makriyalos is a complete contrast. It is a pretty fishing village set on a sandy cove between two rocky headlands with a gently sloping beach which is ideal for children. Walk for 15 minutes and you can find two more good sandy stretches. Windsurfing and watersports are available here in a more natural setting than any other in eastern Crete.

The south coast between Ierapetra and the Bay of Messara is mainly rocky, but it does have four or five isolated beach resorts which are notable more for their beauty than their sand. The most famous is at Matala, which has a greyish sand surrounded by rock caves where early Christians are said to have hidden and buried their dead. They were certainly occupied by hippies in the 1960's, but nowadays the village has developed a series of hotels and likes to coral its visitors into them or the nearby camping site.

The other beaches are at Arvi, Tsoutsouros, Lenda and Kali Limenes. They are all small villages with a couple of tavernas and the most fascinating is Kali Limenes, although it is a long drive from Mires, and its beach is pebble, it is long and spectacular and has a pretty village nearby with a mysterious little island in the bay where NATO submarines refuel. It is also the place where Saint Paul landed on Crete . Well worth the drive in my view.

Nightlife on Eastern Crete

All four of Crete's big towns have a big selection of restaurants, bars and cinemas and a sprinkling of discotheques.

Heraklion is far from the prettiest town by day, but by night it acquires a certain glamour as its squares, alleyways and garden restaurants light up for the evening trade. There is plenty of activity around the cafés and restaurants of Platia Eleftherias by the archaeology museum and Platia Venezelou, while music can be heard in the cellar bars of narrow streets off Dikeosinis. There are also three or four discos near the middle of town.

But those who prefer to eat and drink cheaply without music should hunt the streets between the Venetian port and the market which are lined with good cheap restaurants spilling out on to the pavement.

Agios Nikolaos also boasts a good range of nightlife with a more sophisticated look than Heraklion in the open-air cafés, bars and restaurants clustered around the harbour and the lagoon. Here too you can find Greek music and dancing, spilling into discos like the Galaxy, Romeos and the Kastello in the Mirabello Hotel.

Elounda, to the north of Agios Nikolaos, has its own brand of sophisticated nightlife with a handful of restaurants and a disco operating in summer. You can spend many a happy evening searching for the Shepherd's bar from 'Who Pays the Ferryman'.

Other resorts in eastern Crete that feature nightlife beyond just eating out of doors are Matala, Ierapetra, Malia, Sitia, Stalis and Hersonissos. Malia has a string of bars, restaurants and discos, while Hersonissos seems to have been created for night owls. Its main promenade is one long series of bars, restaurants and discos on both sides of the street, aligned so closely that you can fall straight out of one and into another becoming quite confused about what music is playing on the way.

Visitors who value their sleep should make sure their hotel or room is well back from the seafront.

Not to be missed on Eastern Crete

As anyone who has been there will tell you, Heraklion is not one of the world's most beautiful cities, but it has a number of good things in it which make it well worth a visit. It has a super archaeological museum in the city's main square near the Tourist Office and Knossos is in a dusty suburb on the edge of town looking towards the hills in the centre of the island. There are frequent buses from the port.

The museum has the most precious finds from Knossos, including vases, frescoes, ceramics and jewellery, and others from other Minoan sites on Crete. It also has Roman remains from the island. Knossos evokes mixed feelings due to the way Sir Arthur Evans reconstructed its ruins and frescoes with bright paint to make concrete look like wood and colour up pillars, leaving only a few stone steps, big storage vases and the world's first flush toilet in their original state.

Personally, I don't relish the atmosphere as much as other sites like Phaistos and Zakros on Crete and Akrotiri on Santorini, but it has to be seen by anyone interested in archaeology or just plain humanity. The other sites on the island are complementary.

Heraklion also has thick Venetian walls over two miles in length with occasional forts, which you can hardly miss driving in and out of town. You can find the grave of Nikos Kazantzakis, author of 'Zorba the Greek' in the walls since he was agnostic and was denied a church burial. Appropriately for a Cretan, his tombstone carries the message: 'I believe in nothing and hope for nothing, but I am free.'

You can complete the Venetian era with a tour of the Historical Museum of Crete, which is near the Xenia hotel.

Eastern Crete has all the other major Minoan sites, and they all have points in their favour. Phaistos, almost due south of Heraklion, has a magnificent setting on a low hill overlooking the Messara Plain of southern Crete and is a lot more natural than Knossos. It is also within walking distance of the settlement of Agia Triada and only a short drive from the Roman capital of Gortys. Malia and Gournia to the east along the main coast road have less to show of their earlier glory, but Malia has a magnificent seaside location and Gournia the best outline of a Minoan town, while Zakros, latest to be excavated, lies remote on the east coast, but repays a long journey with its evocative remains half in the sea and a pleasant little village to stay in nearby.

Gortys, about 12 kilometres east of Phaistos, is a neatly contained site of the old Roman capital of Crete, which boasts some of the best Roman remains in Greece. It has a pretty little theatre, odeon, the Governor's house and temples. The odeon contains the law code of Gortys written alternatively left to right and right to left.

If you have a day out at Phaistos, Agia Triada and Gortys, it is worth tacking on Matala on the coast nearby for a swim and a look at the caves above the beach, which were inhabited by early Christians.

Agios Nikolaos has no Minoan remains of its own, but it has its 'bottomless lake' or inner harbour and the frescoed 9th century church of Agios Nikolaos, who is the patron saint of sailors.

'Ag Nik', as it is called by many tourists, is a good starting point for the plain of Lassithi with its thousands of tall windmills or water pumps and the Diktean Cave where the infant Zeus is supposed to have been born. It is a short walk from the village of Psychro and a good imagination will reveal Rhea and her infant Zeus among the stalagmites. Another easy evening drive or taxi ride from Agios Nikolaos is the lovely hill village of Kritsa, which contains the splendid Medieval church of Kera Panagia and magnificent wall paintings of New Testament scenes.

Those who like old Monasteries should make for Kroustellania on the edge of the Lassithi plain near Tzermiadon, and Toplou on the Gulf of Sitia on the road to Vai. Toplou is built like a fortress and held out against invading Turks with the monks pouring boiling oil on their attackers.

The road journey along the east coast is spectacular after Agios Nikolaos, as are the roads south through the mountains from Heraklion, the Bay of Mirabello and Sitia. The palm-fringed beach of Vai is unique, if a little wasp-blown, and the road across the Messara plain and on to Ierapetra is also spectacular once you are away from the plastic greenhouses.

Western Crete

Western Crete, which contains the nomos (or district) of Rethymnon and that of Chania, has far fewer 'sights' than the Eastern end of the island and has developed much later and much less than the coast between Heraklion and Agios Nikolaos.

Its road network is also inferior to that of the east. It has a motorway along the north coast as far as Kastelli and three good roads running down between the mountains to the south coast. But the south coast is only served by road for a short way between Chora Sfakion and Agia Gallini and the road down the west coast peters out before it works its way down to Paliochora.

However, this end of Crete has far less high-rise and tourist strip. It also has better beaches. There is no lack of places to see, including the amazing Medieval castles of Frankocastello and Rethymnon, the two incomparable Venetian ports of Chania and Rethymnon, and the Samaria Gorge, which offers a 12-mile walk through a deep chasm from the White Mountains to the Libyan Sea.

Western Crete has a greater sense of 'isichia' – the peace and quiet and escape from the modern world that Greek islands offer better than anywhere else in the Mediterranean. And it has half a dozen charming natural beach resorts in Georgiopoulos, Kastelli, Falasarna, Plakias, Agia Gallini and Bali.

Beaches on Western Crete

Western Crete has more separate beaches than the west of the island, they are better sand and mostly in prettier, less touristy settings. Visitors who value beaches more than archaeological sites should make for this end of the island.

The two main towns of the area, Rethymnon and Chania, have long stretches of good sand reaching right into their suburbs and they go on for miles beyond. Visitors who want to run out of their downtown hotel straight into the sea should choose Rethymnon where the beach runs east of the town, but for sheer expanses of

beach those reaching out to the west of Chania would win hands down because they run on for 20 kilometres as far as the mountainous Spathia or Rodopou peninsular.

A 5 or 10 minute bus ride from the port of Chania will take you to Neo Chora or Agia Marina, which have strings of tavernas, watersports and clean seas when the meltemmi is not blowing hard. Further west there are other stretches at Platanias, Maleme, Tavronitas and Kolimbari, all with hotels, restaurants, beach sports and camping.

There are good alternatives in both towns too. If you take the road west from Rethymnon you quickly reach the wide sweep of Georgiopoulous Bay, which stretches nearly 10 kilometres from the pretty village of the same name and has a wide expanse of comfortable sand dunes to sleep the day away in, a handful of beach restaurants with above-average cooking in which to lunch and plenty of rooms in which to stay.

Similarly, if you head east out of Chania you can find a beach at Stavros on the tip of the Akrotiri peninsular, where Chania airport is sited and there are others along the main coast road around Kalives and Plaka towards the end of Souda Bay.

Georgiopolis and Stavros are both good places to stay, if you want a spell on the beach and don't fancy the big towns. Two other good spots on the north coast west of Heraklion are Bali and Kastelli.

Bali is a tiny, pretty village only 45 kilometres west of Heraklion along the main motorway which you could easily pass by in a hurry, but it repays a stop with three tiny sand coves, a first-class beach hotel and a cluster of good restaurants in the centre of the village.

Kastelli or Kissamos is a spectacular, but quiet, little port in the far west, which has an expanse of orange sand to swim off, a number of good modest hotels and restaurants and occasional ferries to Antikithera and the Peloponnese.

Staying at Kastelli with a car or scooter can be a delight because it puts you within easy striking distance of the west coast of Crete across the spur-like peninsular of Grambousa and that way lie some of the best beaches on the whole island – perfect sand gently shelving into the sea in scenic coves which are nowhere near as crowded as the beaches on the doorstep of the big north coast towns.

Falasarna, immediately across the peninsular, is the Bay of Golden Beaches. There are 4 or 5 separate coves set between craggy rocks with two small hotels and restaurants on tap. But the nearest bus stop is 5 kilometres away in Platanos. The other top spot on a coast that has a number of pleasant shingle beaches and remote places to stay like Sifnari and Kambos is below the Monastery of Chrisoskalitsa and opposite the islet of Elafonissos. You can wade across to the island and pick a cove to yourself on either side in a perfect natural setting spoilt only by a slightly tatty car park and the absence of a decent beach taverna or anywhere to stay nearer than the village by the monastery.

The south coast of Western Crete offers other beach delights. The most famous centres are Paleochora and Agia Gallini at opposite ends of the coast, and both have their disciples and good watersports, but they tend to be more trendy, pebbly and crowded than remarkable for the quality of their beaches. Better yellow sand beaches can be found at Frankocastello, where there are 4 or 5 separate stretches below the famous Medieval castle with some good restaurants, and a short way along the coast around Plakias. The village itself has a good stretch of sand, though it is becoming crowded as the small hotels and restaurants develop around the bay, and there are three others a stiff walk or easy taxi ride to the west at Damnoni, Amoudi and Preveli, which is now served by a couple of restaurants.

In the opposite direction Rodakino has a good sand beach with caves to escape the mid-day sun and rooms in the village.

Chora Sfakion has two or three pretty stretches of pebble. They do not rank as great beaches by those standards, but are worth knowing about if you are taking boats to or from the Samaria Gorge. The same goes for the long pebble stretch and the crowded sand strip at Paleochora, which is also a terminus for boats to the gorge and Agia Roumeli at the foot of the gorge also has a shining pebble beach which has brought great relief to thousands of people who have walked the gorge for 6 or 8 hours on a hot day.

Nightlife on Western Crete

Western Crete is not so strong on nightlife as the eastern end of the island, but both Chania and Rethymnon are lively in the evening, while smaller coast resorts like Paleochora, Plakias, Agia Gallini, Georgiopolis, Platanias and Kastelli run to a little night music as well as a wide range of bars and restaurants.

Nightlife in Chania takes place mainly around the old harbour in restaurants, cafes and bars. There are one or two attractive garden restaurants in the back-street close by and is not hard to find music. There is also a sprinkling of discotheques and traditional dancing at the International Dance Festival, usually held in May.

As an alternative, take a bus or taxi a few kilometres along the coast to Neo Chora, Platanias or Galatas which is the birthplace of Mikis Theodorakis and usually lays on music as a reminder of its famous son.

Rethymnon has a delightful half-moon of fish restaurants along its harbourside and more in the back-streets close by. Here the bouzouki and the hi-fi are more common than the discotheque especially during the local wine festival, usually held in July. But there is one lively disco scene by the harbour in summer and another on the edge of town. Rumour has it that fish costs half as much in this town as in other parts of Crete because the nearby fishing grounds are particularly rich, but check the price on ordering to be on the safe side.

You can find a quieter, alternative night scene a short distance away to the west at Georgiopolis along the main coast road, or even closer at Misiria 4 kilometres east of Rethymnon.

Paleochora, Plakias and Agia Gallini on the south coast all have a wide selection of restaurants along their seafronts and in the backstreets, where music and the odd disco are also to be found.

Kastelli (or Kissamos) is quieter than the other resorts, but has a lively line in restaurants around its main square and many of them serve the local Kastelli and Kissamos wines.

Not to be missed on Western Crete

When you enter Western Crete you wave goodbye to Minoan sites, but not to history. The Venetians left their most splendid towns and castles in this part of the island.

The splendour starts in Chania – formerly Candia and dubbed 'Candy' by Shakespeare. The Venetians chose this beautiful town as their capital and it has remained the capital of Crete, though it has often been called 'the Venice of the East'.

You can see why when you look at the old city walls, the splendid double-harbour the Venetians built, and the tall mansions that lie around it and have now been largely restored after wartime bombing, some as restaurants or small hotels. This is a much more 'together' town than Heraklion with a great sense of unity and style. Even the tourist office has found a special place on the quayside of the inner harbour in the domed Mosque of the Janissaries.

Chania has an archaeological museum with Minoan finds and a historical museum which contains the best relics from the Venetian period down to the present century. It also has the home and statue of Venezelos, the leading statesman.

Rethymnon, the other big town of western Crete is hardly less splendid. It is another Venetian town with its compact harbour sandwiched between a tall, handsome castle and the beach, which is flanked by a palm-shaded promenade. Around the curved harbour are a host of narrow streets containing both Venetian and Turkish houses with wooden balconies.

The Fortezza is one of the best-preserved Venetian castles in Greece, rivalling the Knights' castle in Rhodes town and challenged only by Frankocastello in Crete.

Frankocastello is on the south coast south-west of Rethymnon. It is a smaller castle, but has its own splendour because it stands proud and isolated on the seashore with only a beach and a restaurant for company, in such a good state of preservation that it must look much the same today as it did centuries ago when it was built.

It is believed to be haunted by Greek resistance fighters massacred by the Turks in 1829, who march from the castle into the sea at dawn each year on May 17. See it at dawn or dusk and you may well conjure up a vision of the slaughtered patriots.

Souda, the big port and NATO base east of Chania wins no prizes in the charm stakes, but the Akrotiri peninsular that rises above it is worth a visit. As well as the grave of Venezelos, it has the two monasteries of Agia Triada and Gouverneto and the stalactite cave of Katolikon where St John the Hermit lived. Another huge cave with stalactites and stalagmites can be found at Afrata, a few miles off the main coast road at the foot of the Spatha peninsular.

Kastelli has a castle built on the site of ancient Kissamos and Falasarna across the neck of the peninsular has Minoan remains, but they have to be searched out and neither compare with their competitors elsewhere on the island. The most memorable spot on the west coast is, in fact, the pretty little monastery (or nunnery) of Chrysoskalitissa – or 'golden stairway' – not far from Elafonissos islet.

On the south coast there is a castle at Paleochora, a pretty little wedding cake church at Agia Roumeli, and a handsome war memorial to British troops at Chora Sfakion. All these places could be on the route of people walking the Samaria Gorge.

The whole of western Crete is populated by pretty inland villages and deep gorges, making it a delight to drive down through the mountains on any of the roads that link the north coast with the south, but the deepest and best-known is the Samaria Gorge which stretches down from the White Mountains to the sea at Agia Roumeli and has become a special attraction to walkers.

It is 12 miles long and claimed to be the largest gorge in Europe. Anyone of moderate fitness with good shoes can walk its 12 miles of Castle Dracula scenery – towering peaks, rushing springs and stony pathways – in four-eight hours, especially if they set off on the early morning bus from Chania to the top of the gorge.

Agia Roumeli at the foot of the gorge has rooms and restaurants and motor boat connections along the coast to Chora Sfakion and Paleochora, which also have rooms, restaurants and return buses to Chania, but are worth a short stay.

Even if you get lost in the gorge, you won't be alone. It is well-walked even in mid-winter.

Along the north coast between Chania and Rethymnon, movie buffs may want to visit the hill village of Kokkino Chora (or 'red village') to see where 'Zorba the Greek' was filmed and eat in one of the cafés, which are almost shrines to Anthony Quinn who played the title role.

Georgiopoulos is a good place to linger for a meal or a swim between there and Rethymnon and Bali is a lovely little seaside place between Rethymnon and Heraklion.

The south coast between Frankocastello and the nomos of Heraklion has the Preveli monastery near the welcoming village of Plakias, which has been a great centre of resistance over the centuries and has two silver candlesticks given by grateful British servicemen. It also has Agia Gallini, a small fishing village which has mushroomed into a major resort with rooms and restaurants galore in recent years.

Worth visiting off Crete

It is hard to exhaust the delights of Crete because the island is so big, but there are a number of easy escapes to offshore islets by boat and to other fully-fledged Greek islands by both ferry and aeroplane. The Greek mainland is also near enough to combine with a holiday on Crete, using ferries or planes to transfer between the two.

Crete has around 20 satellite isles and there are ready-made boat trips to half a dozen of them, while you can wade across to Elafonissos off the west coast carrying your clothes, despite the amount of blue separating the main island and its tiny satellite on most maps.

Elafonissos is definitely an islet to make for if you like swimming off little desert island beaches surrounded by sand dunes and a number of nudists with not a beach umbrella or beach taverna in sight.

Spinalonga opposite Elounda in the bay of Mirabello is completely different – a place to hunt phantoms. Up to 30 years ago it was a leper colony and has a deserted old village with creepy creaks and bangs breaking the silence

when the wind is blowing.

It was made an islet by Venetian engineers, who cut a channel to separate it from Crete and built a strong fortress. To such good effect that it held out against Turkish invaders for over 40 years. Nowadays it is easily accessible by caique from Elounda or from Agios Nikolaos, which sometimes takes in another small islet on the way. It has a small pebble beach and tavernas to cater for day trippers.

Another islet which held out for a long time against the Turks is tiny Nea Souda in Souda Bay, which was the last place in Crete surrendered to the Turks. It has a spectacular little fort and is easily reached by motor boat from Souda.

Agia Theodori is another small islet near the coast opposite the seaside resort of Agia Marina in the Bay of Chania. It too was fortified by the Venetians, but today it is worth visiting to see its huge cave and the wild Cretan goat, the kri kri, which is becoming hard to spot in the mountains of the main island.

Dia island, opposite Heraklion, is another barren island which plays host to the kri kri, but is not as easy to get to as it looks from the island capital.

The triangular island of Gavdos, however, is easy to get to if you don't mind a four-hour sea crossing from Paleochora, and is thinly-populated. It is the most southerly island in Greece, and is reputed to have been the island of the nymph Calypso who seduced Odysseus to tarry in the 'Odyssey' on his way home from Troy. It is worth tarrying there today because it is a charming, rockly island with a little modest accommodation, a castle in the Hora and two or three pretty shingley beaches near the port.

You can easily combine a visit to Crete with one to Athens and the Peloponnese, thanks to overnight ferries, which do the journey in 12 hours, and Olympic Airways, which do it in an hour. It is worth thinking about for a classical tour.

It is equally easy to combine Crete with Rhodes for glimpses of two big and contrasting islands, or with Karpathos and Kassos, which lie between Crete and Rhodes. There are flights to Rhodes and ferries to the other Cycladic islands and to Rhodes from all the eastern ports of Crete.

You can also fly to Cycladic islands like Santorini, if you want to do the complete Minoan tour, and Mykonos, if you want to visit a small, gay, sophisticated island in the middle of the Aegean, while the ferries run to Piraeus and the southern Peloponnese from Heraklion, Chania and Kastelli. You can also sail easily to the barren island of Antikithera from Kastelli, but it is not a particularly inviting island. Better to stay aboard and go as far as Kithera.

Once in a while there are ships to both Cyprus and Alexandria in Egypt from Crete, but both involve long journeys.

5. Crusaders' Isle – Rhodes

Rhodes is the island of Apollo, the Sun God, and the Colossus, one of the Seven Wonders of the Ancient World. It is also the Crusaders' isle where the Knights of St John headquartered after retreating from the Holy Land and built a string of castle strongholds to keep the Turks at bay when they attacked the island.

Modern crusaders flock to Rhodes more in the cause of Apollo than that of the Holy Land. The sun shines nearly every day of the year and hot weather shrubs like rhododendron, bougainvillea and hibiscus blossom everywhere along with fruits like oranges, lemons, apricots and figs. The beaches of the island are baked brown by the sun, and most visitors too if they indulge in sun worship.

The Colossus which once bestrode the harbour of Rhodes town now exists only on postcards, having fallen victim to an earthquake in 225 BC, but Rhodes has a strong historical background and sites to match. Apart from the Crusader castles dominating Rhodes town, strung along the hilltops of the east coast as far as Lindos and the west coast as far as Monolithos, the island boasts four ancient cities, Lindos, Kamiros, Ialyssos and Rodos.

The island vies with Corfu in natural beauty. Although it is browner and less lush in appearance, it has a painter's landscape with pine-clad hills and mountains rising in the interior around the 4,000 foot peak of Mount Ataviros and white villages sprinkled around the coast, often in grand bays between high cliffs, like that at Lindos which once provided anchorage for one of the world's biggest fleets.

Rhodes has provided a rich natural setting for many films, including 'Guns of Navarone', 'Escape to Athena' and 'Ill Met by Moonlight'.

Rhodes town itself offers two towns in one, with the old town contained in an amazing state of preservation within the castle walls, and the new town, the loveliest modern conurbation in Greece. A unique blend of Italian town-planning and Greek style, it is rivalled only by Corfu town. Not to be outdone, Lindos is all white like a bride in her wedding dress crowned by the most beautiful acropolis in Greece.

There are plenty of cool, green places in the interior of the island, where pinewoods and valleys are fed by streams and olive and cyprus trees grow in profusion beside fruit farms. The new town is also green with pine, plane and blossom trees lining its broad avenues and waterfront, complementing the arched public buildings and grand harbour, legacies of the Italian occupation which lasted until 1948.

It has been called 'the island of Eternal summer' and boasts an 8 or 10-month season, a good two–three months longer than Corfu and other northern

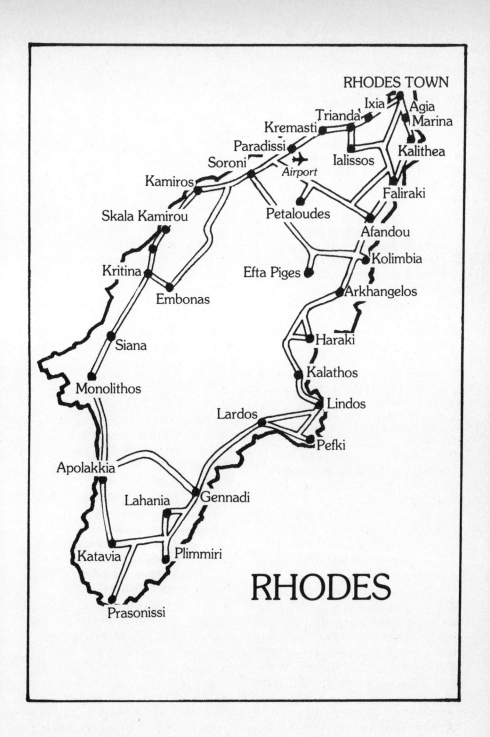

RHODES

islands of Greece. You can swim in the sea in December, if you are determined and don't linger long, and can find over 200 hours of sun in March, half the 420 hour average of June, July and August. With such impressive statistics, you won't be surprised to learn that Rhodes has the best sunshine record in Greece.

The weather, the spectacular landscape and the history are three good reasons why the island draws northern Europeans in droves from Scandinavia and Germany as well as Britain. But Rhodes also boasts long, sandy beaches most of the way around its coast, divinely peaceful places in the south of the island, and modern tourist attractions like tennis courts, a golf course, a casino, nightclubs, foreign restaurants, windsurfing, water-skiing and easy boat trips to its many beaches as well as to other islands in the Dodecanese chain.

Its most popular coastal resorts like Rhodes town, Faliraki, Lindos, Agia Marina, Kallithea, Trianda, Ixia and Paradissi have been transformed in recent years by developments of hotels, villas, restaurants and discotheques to match the rising influx of tourists and the busloads of cruise ship passengers that pour down the coast roads from Rhodes town to Lindos and Kamiros.

Yet Rhodes town remains the only big town in Greece surrounded by a clean, sandy beach and the island has oases of quiet between the big resorts and throughout the south below Lindos in the east and Kamiros in the west. Down there, it is not hard to find a long, broad sandy beach to yourself or to walk alone through unchartered countryside. The only snag is lack of accommodation, which is limited to small pensions and rooms in village houses. The deep south is easily accessible thanks to a ring road 200 kilometres long running right around the island.

Rhodes is cheap for tourists, cheaper than most Greek islands, despite its sophistication, casino and big hotels. It boasts low prices for drink, food products, imported goods and transport like hired motorbikes. They stem partly from the island's duty-free status.

This is the big Greek island with everything. Yet it is not quite so well known as Corfu and Crete to British holidaymakers. It is not surprising that it has soared in popularity in recent years, rising from 15th place to fourth among British package tour destinations, close behind Corfu and Crete.

There are scheduled and charter flights from Britain to Rhodes.

It is also possible to fly to and from Rhodes and other Greek islands, including Karpathos, Kos, Santorini and Crete, each flight taking roughly half an hour.

There are daily ships from Piraeus, the port of Athens, but it can be a depressingly long journey taking between 24 and 30 hours and calling almost everywhere, so it is only for people with plenty of time who want a glimpse of many islands.

The shipping line that runs down the Dodecanese is businesslike, but calls at almost every island, so again time and patience are needed. Fortunately, recent years and calm coastal seas have brought a hydrofoil service to the Dodecanese and island-hoppers should pray that it keeps on running, unlike the central Aegean service which has been withdrawn for the moment in face of rough seas. When last tested, it was running from Samos to Patmos, Patmos to Kos and Kos to Rhodes, taking 1½ hours for each leg, so it more than halves travelling time, yet still gives you a glimpse of passing islands if you brave spray and vibration to travel on deck.

There are also shipping services connecting Rhodes with Symi, Kastelorizo, Halki, the Cyclades and Cyprus that do not always run to the rest of the Dodecanese, and an intermittent service across to Marmaris in Turkey.

Long and broad for most of its length, Rhodes resembles a giant fish in shape with Lindos on its fin. For most of its length it faces the Turkish mainland, though it is too far away to be seen clearly from the island.

Legend says that Rhodes was still rising from the sea when it was selected by Apollo or Helios, the sun god, as his share of Greece from Zeus, the father of the gods, who was distributing it among his children. Apollo named it after his beloved nymph, Rhodos, the daughter of Aphrodite, and the Dorians who ruled the island called their three big cities after the sons of Apollo and Rhodos – Lindos, Ialyssos and Kamiros.

Ancient Rhodes ordered a giant statue of Apollo, its patron and protector, from its most famous sculptor, Chares of Lindos. It stood around 100 feet tall, almost the height of New York's Statue of Liberty, took 12 years to cast in sections and was reputedly mounted with its legs astride the harbour mouth for ships to pass underneath with a torch in one hand to guide them home at night. It is not surprising that it became known as the Colossus of Rhodes and was ranked among the Seven Wonders of the Ancient World.

Alas, the Colossus was short-lived and met an untimely end. It was erected in 290 BC and fell victim to an earthquake in 225 BC. It lay in pieces for eight centuries and was sold off for scrap to a Jewish merchant who carried it off to Syria.

The Apostle Paul came to the island, around 42 AD, and converted many of the Rhodians to Christianity.

The Knights of St John retreated from Jerusalem via Cyprus to Rhodes in 1306 AD and gave the island two more centuries of security, prosperity and relative independence.

The order of the Knights was founded in the 11th century by a family from Amalfi. They never numbered more than 600 and were usually ruled by a French Grand Master. They bought the island from Genoese pirates and won it fully in a long siege of the Byzantine garrison. They then set about ensuring that they would be secure there by fortifying Rhodes town with high walls and building other castle strongholds at key strategic points along the coast of the island and on other neighbouring islands of the Dodecanese. In the town itself they built a hospital and eight inns, representing the eight 'tongues' of the order – those of France, England, Germany, Italy, Castile, Aragon, Auverge and Provence – who each had a portion of the city walls to defend.

They did their work and their fighting so well that they managed to keep the Turks at bay for the next 200 years, including two particularly determined assaults in 1444 and 1480. But they were finally unseated in 1522 when Suleiman the Magnificent was so angry that the Knights were attacking

41

Moslem pilgrim ships that he laid siege to the island for six months with a huge force. Although he lost 50,000 troops, Suleiman finally persuaded the Knights to surrender and allowed the survivors to move on to Malta.

The Italians ruled from 1912 to 1948. They were not welcome as occupiers since they tried to suppress the Greek language and the Orthodox church, but they did give a start to tourism, beautified Rhodes town with noble civic buildings and built good roads. Their legacy is evident today in the new town, while the ghosts of the Knights ride through the old town and stalk every hilltop citadel on the island. Little remains of the Turkish occupation other than two or three small mosques and a fountain in the old town,but there is plenty to see of the ancient Greek cities of Rhodes, Lindos, Kamiros and Ialyssos. This unique combination makes Rhodes a fascinating island for sight-seeing without peer in the whole of Greece.

Beaches

Rhodes is almost one long beach. Even Rhodes town at the northern tip of the island is surrounded by sand and it runs on for bay after bay with a few exceptions right to the southern tip of the island, but the west coast is a lot windier, more shingley, and there are places between Skala Kamiros and Apolakia where the coast is not easily accessible.

The town has good sandy beaches on both sides of its promontory and they are enough to satisfy many of its summer visitors, who crowd together beneath colourful beach umbrellas in serried ranks only a few yards away from their big hotels and the restaurants where they take lunch and dinner. It is an easy life and it

stretches along as far as Mandraki Harbour on the east coast and for three or four kilometres to Ixia on the west side with windsurfing, water-skiing and pedaloes on the calmer stretches. But there are greater treasures, and calmer seas, to be found further down the east coast for those prepared to travel.

The first resort that is separate from Rhodes town is Agia Marina, which has a passable beach with watersports, then comes Kallithea, a thermal health spa with waters that are believed to work wonders on internal problems and rheumatism. The Italian-built spa buildings have seen better days, but the waters are still there and the bay offers good swimming and windsurfing. Lew Grade turned the spa into a German prisoner-of-war camp for 'Escape to Athena'.

You can swim most of the way around the bay of Kallithea as far as Faliraki, which has a superb long stretch of sand beach and is fast growing from a small fishing village into the major beach resort of the island with a healthy strip of hotels and restaurants. Many people now stay here as an easy, quiet alternative to Rhodes town since it is only 15 kilometres down the coast, is slightly cheaper, and boasts calmer, clearer waters. It too has all the watersports.

You can swim too in the bay of Afantou as far as the promontory of Kolimbia, though it is better known as the island's golf course and tennis centre. You can find 18 pearly green holes, tennis courts and professional coaching in an away-from-it-all setting just 22 kilometres from Rhodes town and about 7 from Faliraki.

Kolimbia, a couple of kilometres off the main road – turn by the hospital –

is special. A promontory with sandy beaches on both sides that opens up into a sandstone crater into which the sea floods at high tide. It offers a choice of swimming and windsurfing plus a few rooms and three or four restaurants in a spectacular setting about 30 kilometres from town.

Tsambika is different again – a broad stretch of brown sand with big cone-shaped rocks – and Stegena has a tiny toy-like harbour with a beach beside it, then comes Haraki. It is a pretty fishing village which has two of three separate beaches like Kolimbia, though not so grand, one doubling up as a harbour, a reed-fringed stretch to the right and another to the left of the village. The third beach is overlooked by Feraklos castle, which was a stronghold of the Knights of St John, and the skeletal remains of a Typaldos holiday village started when the cruise line was at its zenith in the mid-sixties, then abandoned to the elements like a modern monument.

The beach to the right of Haraki runs on and widens out to become the big sweep of Vliha Bay with a couple of beach hotels and restaurants at the far end between the pretty villages of Kalathos and Lindos.

Lindos is a jewel – the single most spectacular place on the island and the second biggest town after Rhodes, thanks to its dazzling white houses, winding streets and magnificent acropolis, but it lacks for nothing by way of beach. Again there is a three-way choice; the main sandy sweep of Lindos Bay with beach umbrellas, windsurfing, water-skiing and pedaloes below the town; the tiny enclosed bay of St Paul on the back side of the town and its rocky acropolis, which looks like a lake with two small strips of sand until you descend and see the

break in the rock wall where the sea floods in; and a fair walk beyond the bay of St Paul, there is a long swimmable stretch of sand between the villages of Pefki and Lardos.

Between Lardos Bay and the southern tip of the island the coast road offers an expanse of almost continuous beach, interrupted only by exotic rocks, which split it into coves all the way down to Plimmiri. Genadion is developing into a small resort on a particularly wide stretch of beach halfway down and Plimmiri itself has a modest taverna with a few rooms and a beautiful curving sandy bay beneath an abandoned Italian village. Beyond Plimmiri the tarred ring road becomes dirt track, but the beaches don't end. Intrepid travellers who penetrate as far as Cape Prasonisi ('green island') will find the cape itself rocky and wild, relieved only by a lighthouse, but a short walk away the dirt track runs into a narrow neck of sand with long, lagoon-like beaches on both sides.

The west coast does not match the east, but it has some respectable beaches by the standards of most Greek islands. You can swim off shingley stretches the whole way along from the main Rhodes hotel strip to Kamiros, at Trianda, Ixia, Tholos, Kremasti, Paradissi, Soroni and Kamiros itself, where there are two pretty restaurants close to the sea.

Skala Kamiros is a tiny fishing port backed by a cliff where the ships sail to the offshore islands of Halki and Alimia, but it has a fair beach with some sand and restaurants and a few rooms to match.

Beyond Skala the coast road runs inland and it is hard to get to the sea, but off the road near Siana a new little resort is emerging at Glyfada. The beaches are pebble, but they lie in a spectacular setting between high cliffs and there are rooms and restaurants to reward those who venture down the dirt road.

The south-east coast beyond Apolakia is as spectacular as any beach of the east coast. The whole 17 kilometre stretch that is known as the Bay of Apolakia is wide yellow sand dunes dotted with bushes and cactus constantly pounded by a foaming surf. It only runs out when the coast road turns east towards Katavia and it is possible to find accommodation either there or in Apolakia.

The southern end of the island is remote, rarely visited by package tours and only seen by a handful of people who do the standard tours from Rhodes to Lindos on the east coast and Kamiros on the west coast, so water-sports are rare down there, as are swimming pools and tennis courts. Those who want sailing and tennis should seek in and around Rhodes town as far as Lindos in the east and Trianda in the west. The Rhodes Yacht Club will advise on sailing and most of the big beach hotels around the town and as far down the coast as Afantou have tennis courts which can be hired by visitors.

People staying in Rhodes town who want to swim down the coast can easily travel halfway down each coast by bus, but need a car or a scooter for further ventures unless they are prepared to rise at the crack of dawn for buses penetrating the deep south. Good alternative transport for an easy passage to the east coast beaches like Kallithea, Kolimbia, Tsambika and Lardos is a boat from Mandraki Harbour.

Nightlife

Rhodes is one of the few islands in Greece that has nightlife on a West European scale, adapted to its hot climate, and Rhodes town is as lively by night as any port in the Mediterranean.

It has a casino in the Grand Hotel, open-air cinemas and discos, hundreds of cafes, bars and restaurants, dozens of nightclubs and cellar discos mostly in the big hotels, a sound and light display in the Old Town, a folk dance theatre, and a nightly wine festival at Rodini Park. There is music on every other street and you are hard pushed to do the same thing on two evenings in a fortnight.

For the casino in the Grand Hotel you need a suit and tie, passport and enough drachmas to match the minimum table stake for roulette, baccarat and black jack. For the 'Son et Lumiere' sound and light show at the Palace of the Grand Masters you need only a vivid imagination to conjure up scenes from the days of the Knights and the noisy siege by Suleiman the Magnificent, which are described in several languages two or three times a night throughout the summer.

Those who like a spot of tradition can also see folk dances performed in local costume at the Folklore Theatre in the Old City Theatre and can sample a large range of local wines – mainly CAIR or Compagne Agricole et Industrielle de Rhodes – at Rodini Park on the outskirts of town beneath Monte Smith. It is a pleasant garden setting with wine barrels and glasses set beneath spreading trees between ornamental ponds on which swans glide to and fro. Slightly surrealistic, especially after the first three or four glasses of different wines.

Any of these activities – and especially

the wine festival – should be combined with a meal at an open-air restaurant. Rhodes town is one of the few places in Greece where trad Greek fare like kebabs and moussaka is offered cheek by jowl with a range of international dishes like pizzas from Italy, smorgasbord from Denmark, gravalax from Sweden, roast beef in the English style and pepper steak in the French. There are many international restaurants and bars or 'pubs' that cater for customers from colder climates in a way that could make them feel at home if they could forget the heat and the cicadas buzzing away in the undergrowth.

There are floating restaurants in Mandraki harbour with Norwegian names competing with the Greek fish restaurants across on the quayside nearer the town and Danish pastry parlours vying with the Greek pastry shops around the market and bus station.

Dining out in the Old Town is a magical experience. Greek food with an occasional Turkish influence, tables set beneath trees or in alleyways, and lights reflecting off the high walls and cobblestones of a Medieval city. It tends to be cheaper than the new town too. Finish off with ice-cream or a sticky Turkish pastry and a cup of thick Greek (or is it Turkish?) coffee that looks as though it has been stewing from the time of Suleiman.

If you have started off the evening eating out, you may like to follow it up with a foreign film shown with Greek subtitles or a Greek film dubbed with English. Or a disco/nightclub with an exotic name like the Sultana, the Sphinx, the Aquarius, Vikings, the Zig Zag, Kastro, the Can Can or Elli. Or join in traditional Greek dancing in a backstreet restaurant. Many of the big

hotels have such nightspots.

You can find the same kind of scene, but on a much smaller scale elsewhere on the island in places like Faliraki, Kallithea and Lindos, where there are a number of smart bars, pubs, cinemas and discos. But elsewhere nightlife is the more Greek mixture of eating out in a moonlit taverna and taking an ouzo by the harbourside watching the late fishing boats departing or coming home. Discos are not common in the villages where peace and quiet is the order of the day and night.

Rhodians are, in fact, becoming more image-conscious and are starting to put curbs on areas thick with discos after complaints from visitors that they cannot sleep with their windows open while two or three bars and discos are advertising their presence with loud music. The National Tourist Organisation is working with locals to ensure that they do not go over the top in the cause of providing night-time entertainment. It is just as well because there have been problems in some echoing parts of the new town in recent summers.

Not to be missed on Rhodes

Rhodes is a great island for sight-seeing. There are delights all over which are guaranteed to raise the eyebrows of the most jaded world-travellers. If you set aside a day or two out of your holiday to see the sights, you will not regret it and can always take in a beach or two on the way.

Most people will make first for Rhodes and Lindos and rightly so, but where should they start in Rhodes, which boasts two towns in one plus the ancient city of Rodos on Monte Smith hill on the outskirts of town and three harbours to match? It is a good idea to start walking from the promontory of the new town along the harbourside and to go from there to the Old Town.

On the promontory itself is an aquarium, where you can check up on a number of the fish you can see snorkelling in the clear waters around the island, and a few big ones that you won't want to encounter. The same building houses a museum with freaks of nature like a five-legged goat or two-headed calf.

You will soon reach Mandraki, the first of the three harbours. Its entrance is no longer guarded by the colossus, but by statues of a tiny stag and doe on high plinths, said to protect Rhodes against snakes since the time when deer were brought to the island at the behest of the Delphic oracle for that purpose. The far harbour wall supports the fort of St Nicholas built by the Knights to help defend the town against Turkish assaults and the remains of three windmills, which once worked in the corn trade alongside the wooden ships that moored in the harbour to load up.

Nowadays Mandraki is filled with yachts, fishing boats and small cruise ships that ply along the coast and do day trips to nearby islands and to Turkey.

The town side of the harbour is a tribute to the Italian occupation with a square of striking civic buildings constructed of smooth fawn bricks, which house the Governor's palace, the town hall, the post office, the National Theatre and other offices. Beside the palace is the new town's Mosque of Mourad Reis, called after a Turkish pirate.

The National Tourist office is beyond this square and Makariou Street, but there are signs pointing the way and it is clearly worth a visit to arm yourself with maps, tourist leaflets and programmes of local theatres, cinemas, sound and light displays, wine festival and casino.

You will soon reach the market square and the outskirts of the Old Town, which is flanked by two more harbours, Emborio or the commercial harbour and Acandia, which is used by the big cruise and ferry boats. You can enter the Old Town by one of three gates strung around the harbour.

The Old Town is fresh from the Crusades and the best memorial anywhere to those bloody plundering expeditions and holy wars masquerading as a quest for the holy grail and a free Jerusalem. The Medieval walls of the town, like those of Babylon, are high enough to withstand a fierce attack, thick enough to drive a chariot around and still failed to hold out invaders in the end. They have a number of grand gates and are surrounded by a moat where tiny deer now graze.

Along with the walled harbour, the Palace of the Grand Masters, the street of the Knights with their inns and hospitals, they have all been beautifully restored to the point where they look like a gigantic film set. And they have been used many times in the filming of epics like 'The Guns of Navarone' and 'The Dark Side of the Sun'.

The pebble-paved street of the Knights is straight out of the 14th century except for the glass in the windows and crowds of camera-hung tourists on the pavements. It is lined with the eight inns of the old orders, including the magnificent Inn of France and the more modest Inn of

England, which broke with the Order in the 16th century, but was restored as a building during the brief post-war British occupation from 1945 to 1947.

The Street leads to the Palace of the Grand Masters, which dominates the whole of Rhodes town and contains magnificent halls, windows, furniture and mosaics. It was restored by the Italians after being used as a prison by the Turks and nearly destroyed in a gunpowder explosion in 1856. The upper rooms give great views over Rhodes and its harbours. Nearby is the archaeological museum housed in the 15th century Knights' hospital, an impressive two-storey building which contains the island's most famous statue, the Aphrodite of Rhodes or Marine Venus, statues of other gods and a collection of coins, vases and tombstones.

Walk deeper into the Old Town and you quickly enter the Turkish quarter. It has three mosques dominated by the Mosque of Suleiman, built by the conqueror of Rhodes, which still holds services. In this area you can also see the old Turkish baths, library, bazaar and many houses with old Turkish-style wooden balconies.

Closer to the harbour is the Jewish quarter, much reduced since the German occupation during the war, but commemorated in a pretty way by the fountain in the Square of the Jewish Martyrs. It is a round structure inlaid with coloured tiles and topped by three bronze sea horses.

After this walk you will have missed few of the sights of Rhodes Town, other than a little zoo with more tiny deer, which you pass on the way out of town.

Most visitors who leave Rhodes town to tour the island head for the Valley of the Butterflies and the four ancient cities of Kamiros, Ialyssos, Rodos and Lindos. The Valley of the Butterflies, or Petaloudes, is inland from the airport on the west coast and is a green valley of streams, bridges and waterfalls where thousands of orange moths come in summer to cling to the underside of rocks and bushes and feed on the resin of the thorax trees. They fill the air at the sound of footsteps or clapped hands.

Petaloudes is on the road to Kamiros and Ialyssos, two old cities on completely contrasting sites. Kamiros is set in a cool pine glade close to the shore about 33 kilometres along the west coast and offers the impressive layout of a 3rd century BC city with a Temple of Apollo, market, streets and houses rather in the style of Pompei or Ephesus.

Ialyssos has less ancient remains to show, but is sited nearly 1,000 feet above sea level a few kilometres from the airport road. It has the remains of a Doric temple of Athena and a 4th century fountain set in a glade of cypress trees and also the 14th century church and monastery of Our Lady of Filermos with pretty gardens and an underground chapel. Ancient Rodos, set on Monte Smith hill on the immediate outskirts of Rhodes, and within walking distance of the centre, boasts a stadium, a theatre and another Temple of Apollo. It has few of the splendours of its proud past, but is curious for its name. It is called after the British Admiral Sydney Smith who used it as a lookout post during the Napoleonic Wars. The theatre has been restored to the point where it sports perfect rows of white marble seats.

Lindos is the place for superlatives. It was the most prosperous of the three old cities from around 2,000 BC to 408

BC and today is the outstanding site as well as the unchallenged second town of Rhodes.

A dazzling white town of cubist houses and villas – but, mercifully, no hotels – clings to a hillside above a broad sandy bay which once harboured the biggest fleet in the Mediterranean. It is surmounted by the most spectacular acropolis in Greece.

The temple ruins may not quite match those in Athens, but the setting more than makes up for it. It gives a bird's eye view of the Bay of Lindos and the Bay of St Paul on the other side of the rock, where the Apostle is said to have landed on Rhodes. It looks like an enclosed lake from that vantage point.

The cliff face of Lindos was used to house the big guns in 'The Guns of Navarone' and the film kept the donkey drivers of Lindos happily employed for months carrying equipment up the steep steps of the town to the acropolis. Now their sole traffic is tired tourists, who don't fancy a climb of 400 feet in the heat of the day and succumb to the overtures of the donkey drivers in the little donkey park just beyond the main square of the town.

The best time to visit the acropolis is not at noon when tour buses pour down by the dozen from Rhodes Town, but early in the morning or late in the evening when there is a rising or setting sun to light up the scene and it is not uncomfortably hot to hike up the steps.

Pause on the way to look at the 15th century Church of Panagia, with its rich frescoes and pebble-dash floors inlaid with black designs, the old theatre of Lindos at the base of the

town, and also the 2nd century BC trireme carved in the rock face at the entrance to the acropolis. You then enter the great gate of the Castle of the Knights, with its stairs, grand palace, dungeons and battlements. Today it guards a complex of portico, stairs and propylea leading to the holy of holies, the 4th century Temple of Athena perched on the edge of the cliff.

Many visitors staying in Rhodes and visiting by cruise ship make the bus trip to Lindos. The pity is that they see so little of the rest of the island. You really need to hire a car or motorbike for a day or two to do the whole circuit, perhaps using Lindos as a base. There are plenty of good quality rooms in the town and a little out of season it is easy to rent a villa with bathroom, kitchen and walled garden. The first notes for this book were made in such a place in a windy week in October when it was hard to keep paper straight in a typewriter and the view was too distracting for proper concentration.

From Lindos it is a short drive to the lovely white inland village of Archangelos with its two fine churches, 15th century castle and the monastery of Tsambika close by, to Efta Piges (or 'seven springs') where there is a restaurant, a waterfall and a small lake whose waters feeds the coastal village of Kolimbia, and to the pretty harbour of Haraki with the castle of Feraklos nearby.

A few kilometres inland from Lindos lies another pretty cool spot, the village of Lardos, which boasts pleasant rooms and restaurants in garden settings.

The deep south beyond Lindos and Lardos is beach country, but also worth visiting for wild unspoilt stretches of countryside stretching all the way to the lighthouse of Cape Prasonisi ('Green island'). It is possible to motor as far as the narrow neck of sand that separates the lighthouse rock from the main island, but usually best to complete the last part of the journey on foot. This area is not penetrated by the orange buses that run around the ring road of the island and usually depart at dawn and dusk.

The villages of the south like Genardion, Plimmiri, Katavia and Apolakia are all pretty and not much visited. All have rooms and restaurants in picture postcard settings, by the seashore in the first two villages and around village squares in the other two.

The road along the west coast offers quite different scenery, but no less spectacular, between Kamiros and Apolakia. The outstanding sight of this area is the castle of the Knights at Monolithos ('lone rock'), perched above a deep 800 foot gorge, looking totally unassailable and offering amazing views for those who make the crossing by narrow path without suffering a bad case of vertigo.

There is another castle near Kamiros Skala, a pretty port with boats to the offshore isles of Halki and Alimia, and Kritinia and Siana are inland villages worth visiting.

Between the two there is some good walking from Embonas up and around Mount Atavios, which has a temple of Zeus near the summit. The pine-covered slopes around Mount Profitis Ilias also offer good walking country.

But always leave plenty of time for inland trips and take a good map of the Clyde Surveys type. The roads are poor and wind through thick pinewoods. Signposts are few and it always takes twice the time you expect to drive between two remote villages. It can also be cold on a scooter outside the summer months.

Worth visiting off Rhodes

Rhodes is the main gateway to the Dodecanese, thanks to its international airport; Kos is the only other island in the group with that facility and inbound flights are nothing like so frequent as to Rhodes. You can easily travel by island steamer to any other island in the chain and there are regular day boats to Symi, Halki, Kos and Marmaris in Turkey.

There are also local flights to Kos, Karpathos and Crete and summer hydrofoils to Kos, Kalymnos and Patmos. So it is easy and tempting to take a day or overnight trip to another island for a change of scene if you have a week or more on Rhodes.

Craggy Symi, with its seaside monastery, quiet Halki, Kos, looking like a miniature Rhodes with its grand harbour and towering Castle of the Knights, Patmos with its imposing monastery and cave of St John, and Nissiros with its steaming volcano, all beckon alluringly for day trips. Karpathos and Crete are both easy steps on a touring holiday with a view to seeing another island offering a complete contrast to Rhodes, while Marmaris offers a glimpse of a different country and continent.

Be chary, though, of trying an excursion to more remote islands like Astypalea, Kastelorizo and Tilos, unless you have time to spare, since they can involve long sea voyages and don't enjoy the luxury of daily steamers.

6. The Healer's Isle – Kos

Kos has rocketed on to the tourist track in recent years, and now ranks fourth in popularity among Greek islands after Corfu, Crete and Rhodes. This has resulted from an international airport and a range and appeal similar to, though on a smaller scale, than, its bigger neighbour Rhodes.

It has a pretty, Italian-style port with a Castle of the Knights, sophisticated eating and drinking at cheap prices, easy access to other Dodecanese islands, and long sandy beaches, notably along the east coast at Kardamena and Kamares and on the west coast at Tingaki and Mastihari. It also boasts fascinating archaeological sites in Kos Town and a few miles away at the Asclepion where Hippocrates, the most famous healer of the ancient world, taught medicine.

Kos has a verdant interior which supports a wealth of fruit trees, olives and vines, protected by high hills. It helps to support the story that Kos lettuces originated on the island.

Kos town is neat, clean and cheap – a legacy of the Italians and the special customs status granted to most of the Dodecanese islands.

Local wines and spirits come in big bottles at agreeably small prices, which may explain why the town seems so vibrant with atmosphere and activity at night.

The layout of the town is most pleasant with cool gardens and cafés strung along the promenade, flanked by sandy beaches on one side and a magnificent curve of harbour on the other. It has a mosque dating back from the days of Turkish rule, and a small Turkish community, which is a reminder that the island is one of the most eastern in Greece and is tucked in the lee of the Turkish mainland. It also has a plane tree hundreds of years old of enormous girth beneath which Hippocrates is supposed to have taught medicine.

Kardamena has emerged as the island's main resort over the past ten years, thanks to an endless sandy beach and its close proximity to the airport, which is about 15 minutes away by car, bus or taxi. In the 1960s it was an abandoned fishing village with boat trips to the nearby island of Nissiros, but now it is a long strip of hotels, bars, discotheques and restaurants. It lacks the squares and trees of most Greek villages, but still has charm.

Kos is superbly served by transport – air links with Athens, Rhodes and overseas, ship connections with Rhodes and the other Dodecanese, summer hydrofoil links with Rhodes and Patmos and local boat trips to Nissiros, Pserimos and across the narrow straits to Bodrum in Turkey, though that trip is costly and the boat sometimes hard to find.

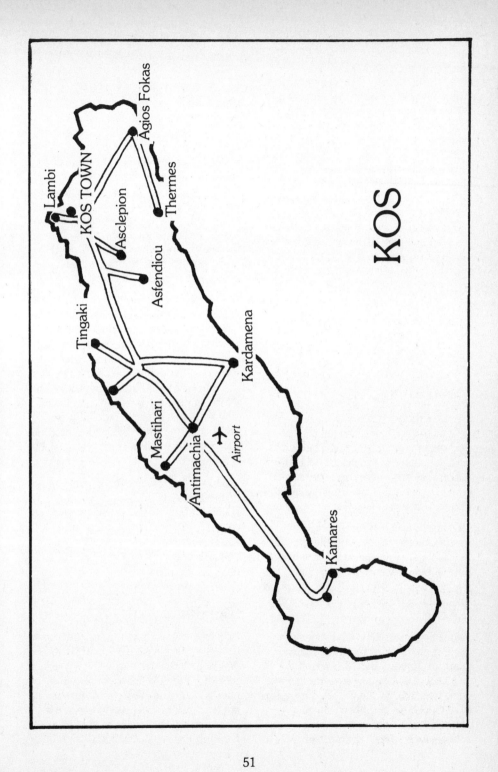

KOS

Lambi
KOS TOWN
Asclepion
Agios Fokas
Thermes
Asfendiou
Tingaki
Mastihari
Kardamena
Antimachia
Airport
Kamares

Kos flourished in the ancient world as a school of medicine, under Hippocrates from 460 BC. He taught mainly under an enormous plane tree in the town – probably an ancestor of the one that marks the spot today – and also 4 kilometres away in the countryside where you can see the ruins of the most famous Asclepion in Greece. The Asclepion was built after his death in 357 BC when Kos was becoming a rich trading nation and used by the Asclipiades, an order of priests who practised medicine by his method using herbs from the hillsides and healing waters.

Beaches

There is an abundance of sandy beaches on both sides of Kos town, stretching towards Lambi in the north and Agios Fokas in the south. In fact, the strip that fronts the town to the right of the castle is as good a beach as you see on many Greek islands and it has all the watersports – windsurfing, water-skiing and paragliding. But the setting becomes wilder and more secluded the further you travel from town and there are some pretty spots within easy cycling distance in both directions.

Go past Agios Fokas, which is a mushrooming resort complex, as far as Thermes and you will find a hot pebble beach washed by thermal waters, which are reputed to be good for aches and pains, along with a spa and café.

There are other sandy beaches within cycling distance of town on the north coast at Tingaki and Marmari if you don't mind the heavy seas that often wash this side of the island. There is a third beach on the north shore at Masthari, but that is more of a car, scooter or bus ride than a gentle

morning's cycle. All are surrounded by pleasant little resorts with restaurants and hotels.

But the best beaches on Kos are on the south coast where the sand is finer and the seas usually calmer. This is one big reason why Kardamena has developed into a thriving beach resort in recent years. Its beach boasts fine sand and runs for many kilometres in each direction, giving a good choice of watersports for those who want them and more isolated spots for those who want peace and quiet with only the waves for company. The village also has a wealth of restaurants and bicycles, cars and scooters for hire.

One of the best beaches on the island is further west at Kamares – which is also called Agios Stefanos after an ancient church on the seashore – 6 kilometres from the hill village of Kefalos. There are sand dunes to laze in, pine trees to take shade under, and a fishing port for local life and lunch. The only threat to this idyllic scene comes from a huge Club Mediterranee complex which is developing close by the church.

Another lovely little beach is the 'Bubble Beach' just south of Kardamena, which can be reached by regular caiques from the harbour. It too has fine sand, dunes and a bit of shade for those who don't want to roast in the sun.

Nightlife

Kos town has a heavier concentration of nightlife than its neighbour Rhodes. A string of tavernas fronting the harbourside compete with an array of dishes and music against a number of smart outdoor bars along the same strip, and there are more restaurants flanking the seashore both north and south of the harbour for those who prefer a quieter scene.

The best fish restaurants are to the north of the harbour and they are unique in the whole of Greece in the way they display their dishes, or plastic replicas, in glass cases outside their front doors. In some of them you can dangle your feet in the sand and watch the big ships to-ing and fro-ing at the entrance to the harbour.

The town centre scene is lively, especially around the square, but it does go quiet around midnight. Then late revellers have to make for the edge of town where nightclubs and discos like the Kahlua and Heaven have bouzouki and dance music into the early hours.

Kardamena is quieter than Kos town and relies more on the traditional Greek nightlife of dining out and drinking under the stars. But there are now two discos at each end of the village, which offer western and Greek music in summer, as well as a number of lively bars with music. The best restaurants also tend to be a short way away from the centre of the village.

Other resorts like Tingaki rely on friendly restaurants and bars for nightlife.

Not to be missed on Kos

Kos town is a delight to look at and walk around. In an hour or two – or even less for those in a hurry – you can see a well-preserved Castle of the Knights, a colourful harbour dating from the same era, a Turkish mosque, a British-style tearoom, a covered market overflowing with fruits and vegetables, a small museum, the plane tree where Hippocrates is reputed to have taught medicine, and the remains

of a major Graeco-Roman town. All are linked by handsome tree-shaded streets.

The old town is in two parts and contains an odeon, an ancient gymnasium, a big marketplace and many temples. Yet it is left casually in the middle of the town for visitors to wander over. Anywhere else the town council would quickly have fenced it off and charged an entrance fee, so see it now while it is so attractively open and casual. It looks more like a public park than an archaeological site.

The Castle of the Knights is set in magnificent gardens ablaze with blossom and shaded with tall trees, and contains marble statues, pottery and old cannons. It is only a short step to the legendary plane tree of Hippocrates, which is supported by stones and wooden props, and looks suitably gnarled but can only be 300 or 400 years old.

Bicycles and scooters can easily be rented in town and the island has good roads. Many places are within a day's cycle ride and the Asclepion within half an hour's pedalling distance. The ancient healing centre, built after the death of Hippocrates, is in a cool green setting in the hills 4 kilometres from town and has a good view of the Turkish mainland. It is a remarkably well-preserved terraced building at the end of an avenue of cypress trees, which has the remains of Roman baths, a hospital and a fountain where healing waters have been flowing for at least two milleniums. It is surmounted by thin pillars and temples, mostly dedicated to Ascelpios, the God of Healing.

Kardamena, around 36 kilometres from Kos Town, is a little far for cycling, but is itself a good centre to cycle to the nearby castle of Antimachia towering above the hills inland as another monument to the builders of the Middle Ages. There is a third castle at Palio Pili between Kos town and Kardamena and it is also worth visiting the old hill village of Kefalos in the south of the island. The nearby beach resort of Kamares has the church of Agios Stefanos on the seashore.

Worth visiting off Kos

Kos is an ideal centre for visiting other islands. There are regular ships to Rhodes, Kalymnos and Astipalea and regular day excursion boats visiting Pserimos and Nissiros. From Kardamena is the easiest passage to Nissiros.

An even easier way to travel is by hydrofoil when it is running. From the beach beside the Castle of the Knights in Kos town it takes just 1½ hours to Rhodes in one direction and Patmos in the other with a flying view of other islands on the way.

It is also possible to go across to Bodrum on the Turkish mainland for a day, though the small boat in Kos Harbour flying a Turkish flag charges highly for the trip and hardly advertises, so it feels a bit like a surreptitious excursion.

7. Pine-Clad Isle – Skiathos

North of Evia and east of Mount Pelion lies a group of a dozen pine-clad islands called the Sporades or 'scattered isles'.

They have no ancient civilisation and not much history, but they are great holiday isles.

Skiathos is the star tourist attraction of the Sporades. It was always a natural for development thanks to a handsome white port and a string of good sandy beaches which almost ring the island. In recent years its role has been confirmed by a direct air link with Britain and the opening of a host of smart restaurants, boutiques and discotheques in the port, which have made it the premier tourist island of the north Aegean.

Apart from a short road to the airport, the only road on the island is a 7-mile stretch along the south coast, which features a regular bus and is within easy reach of most of the island's popular beaches, hotels, water-ski school and windsurfing. It means that those who want to get away from the crowds can easily do so by taking a boat or walking to the north of the island, or by hiring a bicycle in the town.

Skiathos is easy to get to by air, but can also be reached by bus and boat from Athens via Volos and Agios Konstantinos.

Beaches

The long sandy curve of pine-fringed Koukounaries must be the most photographed beach in Greece, but on Skiathos beaches come, like Heinz canned foods, in 57 varieties and reach most of the way around the island.

Koukounaries is now flanked by hotels, dotted with restaurants, and covered with windsurfers and hired boats, but it is as pretty as ever and offers good swimming. It is served both by the bus and regular boats from Skiathos harbour. Both pass a number of other good beaches on the way, including Megaliammmos, Akladias, Vromolimno, Platanias, Troulos and Maratha.

Beyond Koukounaries, around the western headland, lies more remote beaches like Krassi, Mandraki, Aselinos and Agia Eleni. The so-called Banana Beach serves as Skiathos' main nudist beach.

Lalaria cove, usually reached by boats, from the port that go around the island, is the most exotic-looking beach on Skiathos. It is a curve of shining white pebbles ending in an open archway of rock which looks like a prehistoric monster rising from the sea. The same boats usually call at Kastro, which has another lovely beach.

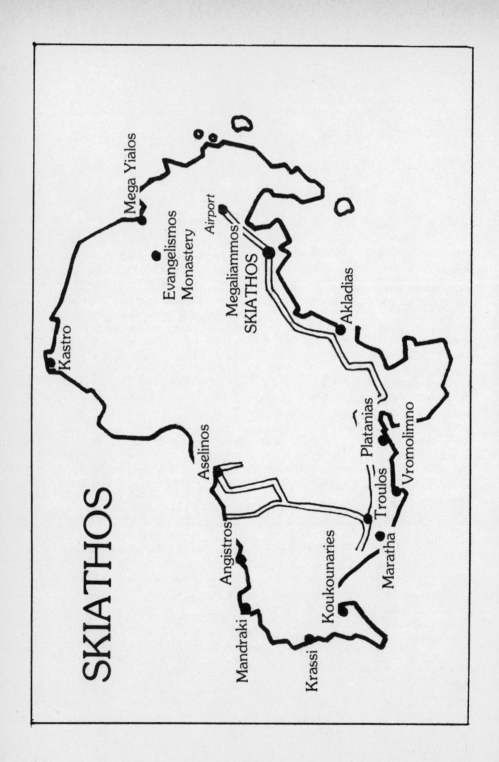

SKIATHOS

Mega Yialos

Kastro

Evangelismos
Monastery

Airport

Megaliammos
SKIATHOS

Akladias

Aselinos

Platanias

Vromolimno

Troulos

Angistros

Koukounaries

Maratha

Mandraki

Krassi

Nightlife

By Greek standards, Skiathos offers sophisticated nightlife in smart bars, restaurants and discotheques around the main port and the pretty green peninsular that juts out into the harbour. Its peninsular sometimes doubles as a disco.

There is a great open-air eating scene on the waterfront and on steps above it and a number of 'pubs' can be found offering a wide range of European beers. The town has cinemas and occasional theatre.

Not to be missed: on Skiathos

A boat trip around the island to Lalaria and Kastro is a must. Kastro is the fortified old town of the island on a high cliff in the north where most of the inhabitants lived up to 1825 as a safe refuge from the Turks and marauding pirates. It has a Byzantine monastery, a church with frescoes and the remains of a castle and old houses.

Those who want to escape the crowds can walk across the island through pine-covered hills to Kastro. It takes around two hours either by the Evangelismos monastery or via Agios Apostolos church and the fountain of Agios Dimitrios.

Worth visiting: off Skiathos

Skiathos has easy ship connections with Glossa on Skopelos and on to the other Sporades. In the other direction ships go to the mainland at Volos and Agios Konstantinos, but the most rewarding trip is by ferry to Platanias on the tip of Pelion for a glimpse of an extraordinarily fertile peninsular with early 18th century villages poking out of wooded hillsides.

8. The Wine Isle – Kefalonia

Kefalonia has opened up to tourism in recent years, thanks to direct flights from Britain, but it is such a big island – bigger, for example, than its famous neighbour, Corfu – that it can easily absorb new visitors.

It has a dozen sandy beaches along the south coast. It is also green, hilly and fertile with scores of red-roofed villages peeping through its pine, cypress and olive trees, three big sprawling ports in Argostoli, Lixourion and Sami in the south and two extremely photogenic ones at Fiskardo and Assos in the north. The three big ports have never quite recovered from the 1950s earthquake which struck hard at the central Ionian isles, but most people stay at the beach hotels down the coast from Argostoli, the capital, or at Poros, a beach resort in the south-east, or Skala to the south.

Sami was the old capital of Kefalonia, or Kefallinia, or Cephalonia – there are half a dozen ways to spell it in English – and was ruled by nearby Ithaca in the days of Odysseus. It is still the main port for steamers from the other Ionian islands like Ithaca and Lefkas, and Patras on the Peloponnese, though some call at Fiskardo. Motor boats from Kyllini on the Peloponnese run to Poros and Agostoli has the airport.

The patron saint is Saint Gerasimos and a third of the boys on Kefalonia are called after him. His body rests in the old church of Agios Gerasimos in the south of the island, which is dominated by Kefalonia's highest mountain, the 5,000 foot Mount Ainos.

Kefalonia's vines and blossoms are reminiscent of Zakynthos and its greenness and grandeur of Corfu. It is not so neat as the other two islands, nor so rich in history, but it beats both, and most other Greek islands, with its wines which are premium brands over Greece. The best-known are flinty-white Rombola and lusty red Manzavino and Calliga, but local wine served by the carafe is usually of high quality and a lot cheaper than the big brands.

Argostoli is an honest, though dull, town with numerous hotels, a good fruit market on the quayside and a road on a causeway across its narrow gulf. Ferries run from the harbour to Lixourion half an hour away across the Gulf of Argostoli, there are regular buses to other parts of the island from the market, and cars and scooters can be hired from shops in town.

The west coast boasts spectacular scenery north of Argostoli where the road is cut into the side of a mountain high above the sea. South of Argostoli is a seemingly endless series of sandy beaches.

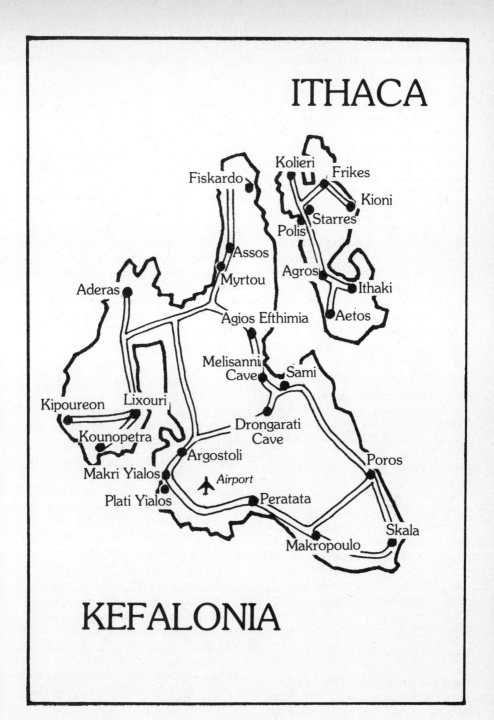

ITHACA

Kolieri
Frikes
Fiskardo
Kioni
Starres
Polis
Assos
Agros
Myrtou
Ithaki
Aderas
Agios Efthimia
Aetos
Melisanni
Cave
Sami
Kipoureon
Lixouri
Drongarati
Cave
Kounopetra
Argostoli
Poros
Makri Yialos
Airport
Plati Yialos
Peratata
Skala
Makropoulo

KEFALONIA

Beaches

Planes from Britain and Athens fly in over some of the island's best beaches along the coast down to the airport 7 kilometres south of Argostoli. Half a dozen sandy coves explain why the island's big beach hotels like the White Rocks and the Mediterranee are sited on this coast on Plati Yialos, Makri Yialos, Livadi and Irina. They also have all the watersports. But there are good beaches in most parts of the island for those prepared to travel.

Along the south coast Gallini and Afrata have pretty beaches with sand and rocks. So do Spartia, Lourdas, Katelios and Skala. On the east coast both Poros and Sami have long pebble and shingle bays, of which Poros is unquestionably the prettier and ringed with good restaurants. Agios Ephimia north of Sami has another passable beach and so does Fiskardo.

But the most spectacular beaches lie on the west coast of Kefalonia. Apart from those below Argostoli, there is a pebble beach at Assos, the prettiest coastal village on the island, and just a few kilometres south are the island's two most spectacular beaches, Myrtou and Agios Kyriaki, which are both long, dazzling white strands backed by high cliffs and approached by the high coast road between Assos and Argostoli. The western peninsular also has a gentle sand beach with first-class taverna at Variko, which is a much better place to stay than Lixourion, and another on its southern tip at Agios Georgios.

Nightlife

Argostoli has lively nightlife, which extends along the coast to the beach hotels and includes two discotheques as well as dozens of restaurants on the edge of town. Poros also has restaurants that put on bouzouki music in season and Fiskardo caters well for diners from the rich yachts that call there.

Not to be missed: On Kefalonia

It is a spectacular island to travel around by car or scooter. The road from Argostoli to Poros is well-tarmaced and runs through the hillside stronghold of Kastro with a well-preserved castle of Saint George, where the island's governor lived in Byzantine times. Then you have a choice of seeing a good collection of ikons at the convent of Agios Andreas or viewing the island's patron saint at the more remote monastery of Agios Gerasimos on the slopes of Mount Ainos.

There is a third grand monastery further along the south coast, called Theotikon Sission, before the road divides right to the pretty harbour and beach of Skala and left through a narrow gorge to Poros.

The road from Poros to Sami is more like a riverbed, but it is driveable and worth the effort because it passes through spectacular scenery and is lined with fruit trees, blossoms and bee-hives that produce the island's crop of delicious thyme-honey.

Sami has developed since the 1950s earthquake, but still has its neat rows of prefabs where people were quickly housed after the disaster. It has a colourful harbour, a developing town and there is a pretty walk around the bay to a café with a goldfish pond by the seashore. Also within walking or easy motoring distance are two of the most spectacular caves in Greece.

Drogarati, 4 kilometres inland, bristles with stalactites and stalagmites in a huge chamber which is occasionally used for concerts. Melissani, on the coast, is completely different. It contains an eerie aquamarine lake open to the sky at its centre and said to be fed by an underground stream running from Argostoli. Strange lights strike through the water illuminating wriggling eels and it could easily have been the inspiration for Homer's description of the entry to the underworld in the Odyssey. You can visit all parts of Melissani in a flat-bottomed boat.

The road north from Sami is again good asphalt and it leads along spectacular high cliffs in the northern peninsular of the island. Both Fiskardo and Assos are worth seeing for themselves since they are the kind of villages that picture postcards and posters are made of. Fiskardo is a classic port, while Assos lies out on a spur of land leading to a peninsular topped off by a well-preserved Venetian castle. Plan to linger there a while.

Lixourion on the western spur is a place you want to get out of, but it is a gateway to some pretty rocky landscapes. The south coast has a rock called Kounopetra, which is said to sway with the tide – and did apparently until the 1950s earthquake – and the west coast has another interesting cave at Drakondi plus the monastery of Kepourio perched high on the cliffs, where there are now only four monks, but they give visitors a warm welcome. Argostoli has an archaeological museum and a short walk inland are the appropriately-named Cyclopean Walls.

Worth visiting: Off Kefalonia

Ithaca is close enough for a day trip by boat. So is Kyllini for a day visit to Olympia. It is possible to island-hop to Zakynthos using Kyllini as a junction, or to use Kyllini as a gateway to any of the other sites of the Peloponnese like Pylos, Epidavros or Mycenae, if you have a car or fancy a mainland bus ride. But it would be best to allow two days to visit Epidavros or Mycenae, since they are a fair distance away and it is a pity to visit such treasures in a rush. You could also take in Delphi by taking a ferry across the Gulf of Corinth.

You can also island-hop to Corfu and Zakynthos by a light plane, which links the three Ionian islands.

61

9. The Flower Isle – Zakynthos

Zakynthos is a stylish green island with an Italian flavour off the western tip of the Peloponnese and south of Kefalonia, which has sprung to fame in recent years thanks to a number of good beaches and a direct air link with Britain as well as Athens.

It was known to the Venetians, who ruled the island for 350 years and called it Zante, as the 'Flower of the Levant' or 'Venice of the East'. It suffered, along with the other central Ionian islands, from the 1953 earthquake, but unlike the big towns on Kefalonia, the main port of Zakynthos was carefully rebuilt on the former Venetian plan with green squares, palm trees and stately buildings in pink and beige.

Zakynthos port is a bustling place, with ferries shooting off to Patras and Kyllini two to three hours away on the Peloponnese. It also has buses to all main villages along the three main coast roads, going south, east and north, and bikes and scooters can be hired. The hill above the town supports the ruins of a fort in which a British force was garrisoned during the Ionian mandate in the 19th century.

The impression of style and fertility sticks on a trip along the south and east coasts – the only ones really accessible by road as the west is high and rocky. The roadsides are often hedged with pomegranate and quince bushes giving way to pine-cloaked hillsides and pale yellow beaches.

The countryside produces some of the best wines in the Ionians, going under names like Verdea, Laganas and Byzantia.

In the springtime and early summer the countryside is a riot of flowers, especially the road north from the port to Alikes and the Argassi peninsular, which yields a fresh picture postcard scene around every bend of the road south to Porto Roma.

Zakynthos also boasts an unusually rich marine life, including turtles, seals and dolphins. Gerakas Beach, which is one of the island's two big breeding grounds for turtles, appeared in David Attenborough's wild-life documentary, 'First Eden'.

The four main resorts of the island are Alikes and Tsivili north of the main town and Argassi and Laganas to the south. They all have a selection of watersports.

Smaller developing resorts are Alikanas near Alikes and Crystal Bay, called after its natural outcrops of crystal at the northern end of Laganas Bay.

Argassi has the twin merits of being within walking distance of town and the gateway to the beautiful Argassi peninsular. It is a miniature Garden of Eden with low hills, pinewoods and olive groves fringed with yellow sandy beaches.

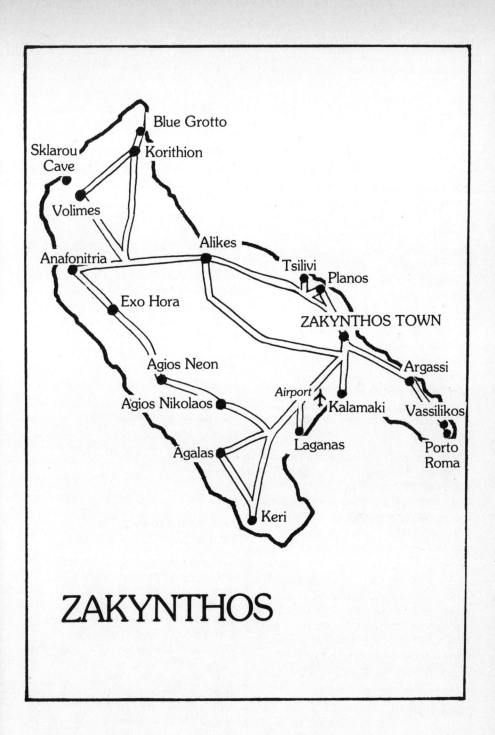

ZAKYNTHOS

Beaches

Beaches line the south coast and south-east peninsular and also occur intermittently along the east coast north of Zakynthos town. The town itself has a small pay beach but Laganas beyond the airport on the south coast is the island's premier beach resort with a broad sweep of golden sand stretching for four miles surrounded by hotels, restaurants and pine trees. It has all the watersports on offer.

Porto Roma and Gerakas at the tip of the south-east peninsular below Vassiliki also have good sand and are more remote from civilisation, yet they have restaurants and an access road from Zakynthos.

Agios Nikolaos has a series of attractive sandy coves, plus one long stretch, which is the single most spectacular beach on the island, while Porto Zoro further north is a tiny developing resort with hotel and restaurant.

There are other slightly less accessible strands in the lee of the south-east cape beyond Vassiliki and nearer town at Argassi and Kalamaki, while Keri in the far south-west corner of the island has a swimmable beach at its small harbour reached 3 miles before the village itself.

Beaches are not so easy to find on the east coast north of the town, but Alikes 11 miles north of Zakynthos has a magnificent stretch backed by a salt lake with two or three beach tavernas. Tsivili, halfway between Zakynthos and Alikes, also has a good beach.

Nightlife

Zakynthos town boasts a dozen good restaurants on picturesque squares and terraces where strolling musicians revive the Venetian occupation at its best with local cantades or folk-songs accompanied by guitar or mandolin. This is a particular delight of Zakynthos which is found on no other Greek island. Try the two restaurants up by the fort for spectacular views of the town, and the beach restaurants along the coast towards Akrotiri for sunsets.

The Panorama restaurant below the fort serves some of the best food on the island in a pleasant garden setting and has superb views of the harbour and town, which looks like an illuminated toy model at night.

The Arekia restaurant along the promenade towards Akrotiri has live music and good cooking. And a restaurant bar on the rocky tip of Akrotiri gives stunning views of the sea and Tsivili hundreds of feet below.

All the main beach resorts have developed a good choice of bars and taverna and are alive with music and discos at night in the summer.

There is also a discotheque in Zakynthos and three or four cinemas.

Not to be missed on Zakynthos

Zakynthos town has four grand churches which survived the earthquake, including the 15th century Agios Nikolaos just off the harbour, and two museums which house other religious relics salvaged after the quake, paintings of the Ionian School and writings of the island's most famous poet, Dionysus Solomos, who popularised demotic Greek, and wrote the National Anthem during the War of Independence. The Venetian castle is a pleasant evening's walk away from town and gives amazing

Samaria Gorge (Crete) —
One of the world's most
spectacular walks

Rhodes Town –
The old town looks down
on the new

Skiathos —
An island of lovely
sandy beaches

Kefalonia —
High, mighty and scenic

views of the island and the Peloponnese.

Visitors staying in the town should take buses or rent their own transport to see the rest of the island. The road along the south coast leads through pinewoods.

Gerakas and Crystal beaches at the north end of Laganas Bay are breeding grounds for loggerhead turtles measuring up to 4 feet. In fact, the Greek Government has had to limit building on a 500-metre strip of Crystal Bay where the turtles lay their eggs to prevent them being harrassed by building, visitors and disco-music. Keri in the south-west has pitch springs which have been famous since the time of Herodotus and is also the centre of a hunting area, which adds spicey rabbit stew and game birds to the menus of the village restaurants in the right season.

The island is renowned for its healing sulphur springs and picturesque caves, which are found mainly along the inaccessible west coast and are most easily reached by boat from the quayside at Zakynthos or from Alikes. The three big sea caves are Agios Gerasimos and Sklavou on the west coast and Kianoun or the 'Blue Grotto' just north of Korithi on the northern tip of the island. There is also the big Megali cave between Kampi and Kallithea in the middle of the island.

A boat ride along the high west coast passes something like 100 caves and also the famous Smugglers Cove.

A short boat ride from Keri harbour takes visitors to the tiny islet of Marathonissi, where turtles breed in relative peace and quiet. The harbour itself has a quota of wildlife like frogs and baby turtles in a limpid stream

and also boasts two good restaurants, so it is worth a visit.

Anyone with a car or motor-bike should make a trip to the north west end of the island. Take in the island's best-known monastery of Anafronitria, the rug-making village of Volimes and the tiny fishing harbour of Korithi. It is short on beach, but long on restaurants in a pretty setting and one of them has a surprisingly good swimming pool overlooking the sea for a pre-lunch dip. Allow plenty of time for this trip as the road is longer than it looks and Zakynthos has more than its quota of pot-holes where drivers least expect them.

Another worthwhile excursion, and a much shorter one, is up to the fort overlooking the town, taking in the pretty, spread-out suburb of Akrotiri where you can find many of the island's finest mansions sited along country roads in a cool hilly setting.

Worth visiting off Zakynthos

There is a regular ferry to Kyllini on the Peloponnese, which makes it easy to visit Olympia or to island-hop to Kefalonia and Ithaca.

There is also an extremely useful island-hopping Olympic plane, which flies to and fro from Corfu via Kefalonia. It is an extremely scenic route with surprisingly modest fares.

Kyllini can also be used as a gateway to all the other attractions of the Peloponnese if you have time and a car or fancy a mainland bus ride. But allow two days to visit the likes of Epidavros and Mycenae since they are some distance away and it is a pity to see them in a rush.

Delphi could also be taken in by ferry across the Gulf of Corinth.

10. The Chic Isle – Mykonos

Mykonos is lively, fashionable, and photogenic, cosmopolitan and well-developed. It has been called the St Tropez of the Aegean and there are connotations because the island caters for nudists, gays and pleasure-seekers. But in a unique Greek way.

It has almost given up farming and fishing in favour of running restaurants, discos, nudist beaches and gay weddings.

It is not a totally unspoilt Greek island and is not ideal for families. Yet it has great charm and can be great fun. It is stunning to look at and has learned to live with mass tourism better than some Greek islands. It is not covered with high-rise hotels and there is little sense of over-development.

Surprisingly, it was little more than a stopover en route for Tinos and Delos in the 1950s, but it was tailor-made for a popular island holiday centre with its dramatic brown landscape, its whitewashed cubist houses, its windmills and its 365 wedding cake churches. There are probably nearer 500 today and many have been endowed by islanders who have become rich through the tourist trade.

In the early days the island had its own rough red wine and a pelican called Peter. You will not find the wine nowadays as agriculture has almost ceased in favour of tourism, but Peter the Second can be seen wandering around the waterfront and sometimes, if you look carefully, you might even catch sight of two pelicans.

The main harbour and the labyrinth of houses behind it make up one of the most spectacular island capitals in the Aegean. It boasts a horseshoe of cafés and restaurants around the harbour and another horseshoe of narrow streets through the town which is lined with trendy restaurants, bars, art shops, and boutiques selling jewellery, fashion clothes, furs and handicrafts.

These are the landmarks of any walk through the maze of streets where it is easy to get lost, even after you have been there a week. Local folklore has it that the town was built that way to confuse invading pirates and you can believe the story after a couple of glasses of wine.

You can live well in the town, with hot showers and sunny balconies in a dozen or more small hotels that have sprung up over the past 20 years, though rooms tend to be more pricey than on other Cycladean islands and it often pays to hunt around on your own rather than taking the first offer you get on the gangplank of an arriving ferry.

There are also a dozen small hotels flanking most of the main beaches around the island and it can make sense to live outside the town in high season if you want to have some choice of places on the beach and

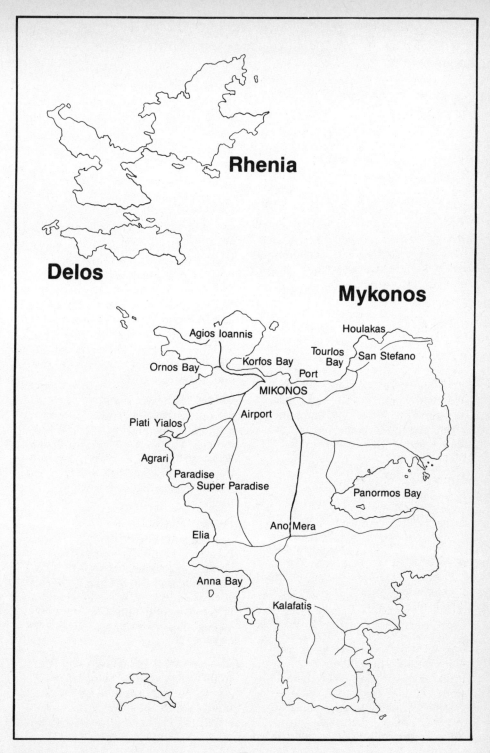

Rhenia

Delos

Mykonos

Agios Ioannis

Houlakas

Tourlos
Bay

San Stefano

Ornos Bay

Korfos Bay

Port

MIKONOS

Airport

Piati Yialos

Agrari

Paradise

Super Paradise

Panormos Bay

Ano Mera

Elia

Anna Bay

Kalafatis

enjoy quiet sleeps, rather than trip the light fantastic every evening. But bear in mind that the hotels on Kalafatis and Agios Stefanos beaches can be expensive, even for the simple things in life like omelette and coffee.

The best choice for out-of-town stays could be Plati Yialos, which offers a choice of accommodation and restaurants, plus a road to town that is just about walkable, and affordable if you miss the last bus and have to take a taxi.

The only sad side of Mykonos is that tourism swells the local population too many times in mid-summer and some of its services groan to breaking point. The buses to the beaches are ridiculously crowded and so are the banks, as though the islanders are trying to squeeze the last penny out of their guests. They don't need to because they thrive on tourism and are visited by some of the richest free-spending tourists to visit Greece as well as back-packers and campers, who can also find places around the shores without too much hassle.

Beaches

The beaches are good, some spectacular, and most of them have restaurants on them. Those away from the town have a liberal sprinkling of topless bathers and two – Paradise and Super Paradise – are frequented by narcissistic nudists, mostly male. The local police usually turn a blind eye, despite notices banning nudism – even where there are loads of lithesome male couples, as on Super Paradise – or they expect bathers to rush into their briefs when they approach and then move away again. People who don't fancy a nudist beach, or one to themselves, can either follow the example of the police

or find as good a beach elsewhere on the island.

There are welcoming sandy beaches on the north, south and west coasts of the island, beckoning visitors to cool off on the many white hot days for which it is famous.

Venture beyond the beach to the left of town and the one in the harbour, unless you want to be in the company of hundreds of other sun-seekers, and in the case of the one on the left risk a bad scratching on the reef close inshore.

You can find good beaches at Elia, Anna Bay and Kalafatis, all a short walk from the inland village of Ano Mera and in the lee of the offshore islet of Tragonissi. There are two other beaches in the Bay of Panormos and Fteila, which can be reached by hired scooter, car or bus via the village and monastery of Ano Mera.

Within a half hour's walk of town there are other good stretches at Ornos Bay, San Stefano, Korfos and Agios Ioannis. The coast along from Agios Stefanos has two sizeable hotels and there is another at Kalafatis, but they tend to charge highly for indifferent food.

Unless you feel embarrassed or prudish, a day out at the Plati Yialos–Paradise complex is a must. It offers six coves of sand in succession, reached either by small boat from the port or hired scooter or by a doddery little bus from the port, which always seems to have standing room only for its 60 to 70 passengers.

The best sand and eating is on Psarou to the right of the bus stop. Plati Yialos has a choice of restaurants, hotels and the bus stop. Paradise, Super Paradise and Elia can then be reached by boat or walking east over low cliffs. They are good beaches with cheap restaurants, serving a variety of couples decorating the sand. Many on Super Paradise are slender young men with a taste for pastel shades and gold chains. Some of them never swim.

Since two equally sandy coves between Plati Yialos and Paradise are often bare of people it is tempting to conclude that Paradise is closer in spirit to Narcissus rather than Apollo.

Mykonos is often windy, thanks to its position close to the vortex of the Cycladic wind system and its lack of high ground, so it often pays to check which direction the wind is blowing before deciding whether to go to the north or south coast to swim.

Nightlife

Unlike so many Cycladic islands, Mykonos has ample nightlife and dozens of places to eat out. You can eat well on a Greek cuisine spiced with spit-roast pork, chicken and lamb, plus a broad spread of international dishes in almost any price range around the golden horseshoe of streets that threads around the town and find speciality fish restaurants like 'The Waves' beneath the windmills and along Mykonos' own 'Little Venice' harbour. Then you have a wide choice of bars and discotheques.

Like many of the restaurants, they are not cheap, but often worth the money. They serve cocktails and expensive wines. They rarely serve retsina and have long ago given up the custom of serving local wines, which have anyway almost disappeared, but drinks can be imaginative and perfectly chilled. The Nine Muses, the Remetso and Windmill are famous, but try the frenzied silvered dance

floor at Piero's for somewhere different to bop or Kastro's Bar for a sophisticated drink.

You can sit high above the sea and study the reflections of the moon or harbour lights across the bay while sipping one of the incomparable Kastro coffees – a variant on Irish coffee – and listening to soft music.

Not to be missed on Mykonos

Mykonos does not have many things to see, apart from its dramatic white port and yellow beaches, but don't miss a visit to the secluded little inland village of Ano Mera and its monastery, which boasts some pretty 500 year-old wood carvings. Nearby around Panormos Bay is an ancient town and Venetian fortress.

The port has a charming little folk museum for wet days and one or two spectacular little wedding cake churches nearby, while the archaeological museum on the road to San Stefano has pottery from Delos.

Worth visiting off Mykonos

The nearby island of Delos is a must for anyone remotely interested in history and archaeology, and can be reached by motor boat from the port, but try to pick a day when the sea is calm.

It is not too difficult to take a bigger ship to Siros, Tinos, Paror or Naxos for a day or two and the island has regular ships and planes to Piraeus and Athens airport as well as Rhodes. But don't bank everything on one ship, especially in July–August when the meltemmi blows hard in the central Aegean.

11. The Windmill Isle – Paros

A jewel of the Cyclades, Paros has developed rather like Mykonos ten years later, but has not become quite so chic, expensive or gay and is in every way a bigger island. It boasts a wealth of sandy beaches, thrusting coastal villages with white houses and picture postcard harbours as well as a handsome main port at Parikia with windmills, and blue-domed churches framed in green hills, vineyards, and pine trees.

Paros lies squarely in the middle of the Cyclades, and its wind system, and enjoys a regular stream of ships from Piraeus which take around 6 hours and go on to Naxos. It also has daily flights from Athens to its new airport; a valley of the butterflies to rival that on Rhodes; bicycles, scooters and cars for hire; and its own wines.

Gentle hills inland surround some of the best vineyards in the Cyclades, producing a variety of flinty red and white wines under names like Lageri, Moulin, Meltemi and Naoussa. They also protect half a dozen coastal villages and as many again inland, which are usually linked by good roads. They include a ring road around the island, which links all the coastal villages, and one main road across the middle of Paros to the east coast via Marathi and Marpissa.

Parikia is a bustling whitewashed town with winding cobbled streets and occasional glimpses of the Parian marble that Pericles and his architects chose for the Acropolis in Athens. It has two campsites and masses of rooms. Life seems to revolve around the quayside where the big ships dock and a windmill serves as the tourist police office and the main bus stop. It has a bus timetable, a list of the main hotels on the island and a sign saying: 'Nudity is forbidden', which everyone ignores.

The town straggles along the coast in both directions, to campsites in the north and hotels in the south. It never seems to run far back from the sea, except for the centre, which is a maze of flower-decked white alleyways reminiscent of the grand maze in Mykonos town and is rich in food, leather, souvenir, paper and pastry shops. It can become crowded with tourists in mid-summer, and rooms hard to find, but Paros is an easy island to get around by car, scooter or the frequent buses from the windmill, which go mainly to Naoussa and Dryos via Marpissa and Piso Livadi.

They run along good roads through low hills, with frequent glimpses of vines, corn and cattle, which give a strong impression that Paros can manage well without holiday-makers, though the coastal villages suggest otherwise.

Naoussa, around 10 kilometres from Parikia and just about walkable on a cool evening, is a gem of Cycladic

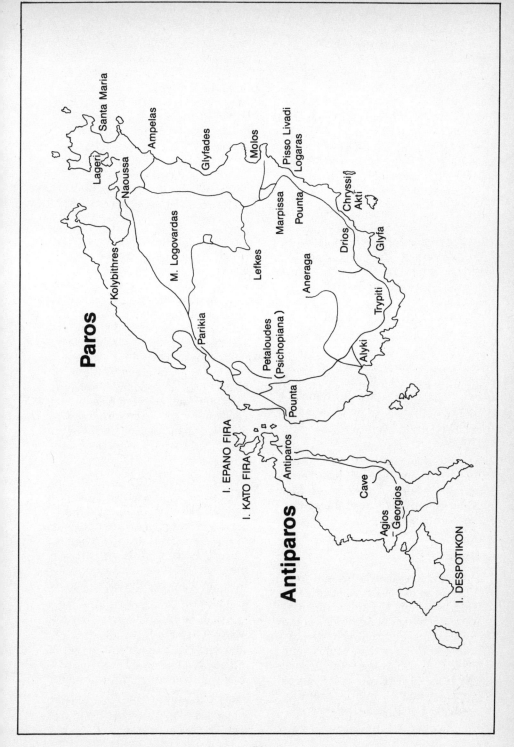

architecture with white winding alleyways, hanging with purple bougainvillea, an idyllic miniature fishing harbour and its own rough red wine, best drunk chilled.

Dryos and Piso Levadi are two smaller resorts on the east coast of the island, with a sprinkling of hotels, rooms and restaurants. Piso Levadi also has a small boat running across the straits to Naxos in summer.

The other major coastal village is Aliki in the south-west, which also has hotels, rooms and restaurants. Pounda on the west coast opposite Antiparos is a tiny place with a hotel and landing stage for boats to Antiparos.

Paros has a firm place in history through its export of Parian marble and also skilled sculptors like Ariston and Skopas who learned their trade on the local stone. It was ruled by the Persians, the Athenians, and the Romans, then the Duke of Naxos and the Turks until the War of Independence.

The island was an early participant in the War against the Turks and also contributed one of its heroines, Manto Mavrogenous, who lived the rest of her life on Paros.

Beaches

Paros today is as rich in sandy beaches as it once was in marble. They start right in Parikia, running around the bay on both sides of the port. Livadia beach, which flanks the campsite north of the town, is better than the beach to the south and gets better the further you walk towards the cape. Boats from the harbour serve the coves nearest the cape.

Naoussa also has a healthy quota of beaches with calm seas around the broad sweep of Naoussa Bay and there are others within easy walking or scootering distance on the east coast opposite Naxos. A good sand beach runs to the east of the harbour, there are small coves near the Hippocampos hotel to the west, and there are more exotic coves across the bay at Kolymbithres, set between smooth grey rocks in odd shapes. Kolymbithres is sometimes served by boats from Naoussa harbour and has a restaurant.

Going east from Naoussa the nearest beach is the sheltered cove of Lageri where you can swim out to a small island. Santa Maria, across the narrow neck of the northern peninsular, has a choice of three sandy curves and Ambelas, easily reached by car or scooter, has another sandy stretch flanked by a hotel and restaurant.

Heading south along the Paros ring road you can find more beaches at Glyfada, Tsoukali and Molos, which has two curves of sand enclosed by a big bay and served by three restaurants.

Molos is within easy walking distance of Piso Levadi, which has a campsite and two beaches, one across the headland that supports the monastery of Agios Antonios and the other towards Logaras. There is a third in the bay of Pounda, the second village with that name on the island.

South of Pounda is the most famous, and most photographed beach on the island, Chryssi Akti or 'Golden coast', which is ripe for development and has already seen some in the shape of hotels and restaurants.

Chryssi Akti is within easy walking distance of Dryos, a quiet little village with two hotels and restaurants to

72

match, which also has its own pine-fringed beach. This area is served by the same bus that runs to Marpissa and Piso Levadi.

There are two quiet shingle beaches around the south coast at Glyfa, which are worth remembering when the island is really crowded in mid-season, and Aliki has its own fine curve of sand, though it is hemmed in by the village. Then there is a respectable, but not spectacular, curve of sand at Pounda opposite Antiparos before the ring road turns inland on its way back to Parikia.

Nightlife

You can dine out in style on this island and find plenty of smart bars and discotheques to round off the evening.

Parikia provides good eating at a dozen restaurants, including some along the seafront, in garden settings in the midst of the village and in the two or three little squares that make up its centre.

Naoussa has a similar variety with fish restaurants around the fringe of the harbour and garden restaurants up the winding streets of the village.

The main bar and discotheque scene is in the middle of Parikia a short way back from the waterfront, where half a dozen establishments compete cheek by jowl and boom out rock and Beatles numbers across the bay.

Not to be missed on Paros

Parikia has the Ekatonda Pyliani, the church of 100 gates perched on high in the centre of the town, which was started in the 6th century AD, though the oldest visible parts date from the Middle Ages. It does not quite live up to its name, but is still a curiosity worth viewing with a huge cypress tree acting as a steeple for the church bells after the last one collapsed in an earthquake. Inside are the bones of the island's patron saint, Theokisti, her hand and footprint as well as some pretty icons.

Near the church is the town's cute little museum, which contains a history of Greece carved out on Parian marble and finds from local temples in the same material.

The buildings themselves are all within walking distance of Parikia with the remains of temples of Apollo and Aphrodite to the north of the port around Livadia Bay and the remains of an Asclepion temple – a temple of healing – and a temple of Apollo south of the port around Souvlia, but they are disappointing.

The wonders of Paros are more modern, and easily reached by the ring road around the island if you have transport. Like the valley of the butterflies (or Petaloudes or Psycopiana), a rival to the one in Rhodes, which is located just off the west coast road between Souvlia and Pounda. It can be reached either by donkey or walking from the coast after taking a bus to Pounda and affords the pleasant sight of thousands of reddish moths swirling around trees and mossy banks in a damp valley, but only for a couple of months each year.

Paros also has a rich quota of monasteries, including Christou Dassos in the wooded area near Petaloudes; Logovardos in a grand position on the Naoussa road, which boasts a wealth of old icons, but bans the fair sex; Agios Theodoros in the south where the nuns do rich tapestries; Agios Georgiou a stiff walk inland from Dryos; Agios Antonios, which sits on a hill beside a Venetian castle between Molos and Piso Levadi; and Thapsanon in a spectacular isolated position in the hilly centre of the island.

Touring Paros is a delight because there is a surprise view of a monastery or white coastal village around every corner and a round tour of the island can easily be completed in a day.

Worth Visiting off Paros

Paros has 17 small satellite islands which can often be visited by boat after persistent enquiry. Kato Fira and Epano Fira have super beaches, as does Antiparos, which makes an easy day trip from Parikia or Pounda. Naxos is only 1½ hours away by ferry and Mykonos, Siros and Ios are all about 2 hours away by direct ship.

So close to the west coast of Paros that you feel you could swim across, Antiparos is the biggest of the 17 satellite islands of Paros and has

blossomed in its own right in recent years.

Its sudden popularity is due to its casual desert island atmosphere coupled with a well-developed main village. There are half a dozen sandy pine-fringed coves within easy reach of the main port, which is an appealing village with half a dozen busy restaurants and a similar number of small hotels, bars and discotheques along the side of a sheltered lagoon-like harbour.

Antiparos is served by 3 or 4 boats a day from Parikia and an occasional one from Pounda directly opposite on the west coast of Paros. They take between 20 and 40 minutes to do the trip and sometimes go on around the island to the cave on the south-east coast and the bay of Agios Georgios on the west coast.

From most parts of the island you have superb views of Paros across the narrow straits that separate the two islands.

74

12. Vulcan's Isle – Santorini

One of the most dramatic events in the ancient world has created one of the natural wonders of the modern world at Santorini – an island which is called after its patron, Saint Irini. It is almost as often called Thira and occasionally Kaliste or 'the most beautiful'.

It could not have looked that way on a fateful day in 1500 BC when volcanic Santorini blew its top. The eruption may have been three to four times the size of Krakatoa in the last century because it left a crater nearly 3 times as big. It landed enough ash and tidal waves on Crete 60 miles away to bury the Minoan cities on the north shore and may have caused the Biblical flood across the Middle East that launched Noah's Ark.

It also launched a legend – of the city of Atlantis sliding into the depths of the sea. And it just could be true because the eruption carpeted the surrounding seabed and beaches with black pebbles and pumice stone, created a sea-filled crater beneath a sheer crescent of cliffs 1,000 feet high and then threw up lava islets in the bay where the volcano still smoulders to this day.

Looking at a map of Santorini and its neighbouring islets, it is easy to imagine that it was once roughly circular in shape with the islands of Therassia and Aspronisi as hills on its western shore and the seawater lagoon around Palia Kaimeni and Nea Kameini in the middle the high reaches of the island.

Thanks to the eruption, Santorini is the single most spectacular sight in Greece, its main town of Thira or Fira perched 1,000 feet above sea level on the lip of the crater and others sprinkled along the spine of the island like crystals of salt. Thira has some of the most scenic accommodation, restaurants and bars in the world hanging along the edge of the cliff with a bird's eye view of ships like toys in a bathtub 1,000 feet below.

Both sides of the island have big drops and also radiate exotic colours, mainly reds, browns, yellows and blacks in layers across bare hillsides, which make it look as though it has been painted by one of the French impressionists, and they make a strong contrast to the olive green eucalyptus trees flanking the roads and the white villages on the clifftops. The white Cycladic dwellings are interrupted only by an occasional blue church dome.

All the island's roads run past black walls and cultivated fields, where the rich volcanic soil of the island is put to good use, notably in vineyards, where the vines are plaited in circular pig's tails to strengthen them against the high winds that blow across the clifftops. Santorini produces juicy sweet grapes and some of the best

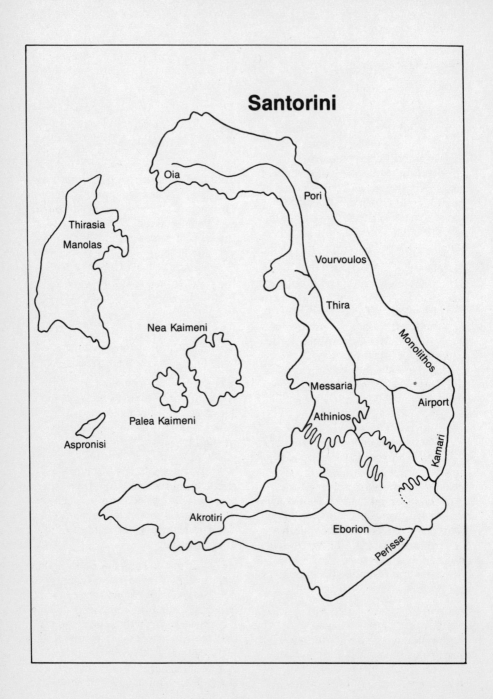

Santorini

Oia

Pori

Thirasia

Manolas

Vourvoulos

Thira

Nea Kaimeni

Monolithos

Messaria

Airport

Athinios

Palea Kaimeni

Kamari

Aspronisi

Akrotiri

Eborion

Perissa

wines in Greece – rich reds, sweet roses and smokey whites – which sell under romantic-sounding labels like Atlantis, Lava, Kaldera, and Vulcan.

It is easy to explore Santorini since there are regular bus services, tours to its many places of interest, and bikes and mopeds for hire in the town. A hired scooter or moped is an ideal way to see the island, since it is the right size for such machines.

Inevitably the island has roared on to the tourist track in recent years. Cruise ships and ferries from Piraeus, Crete, Ios and Naxos pull in daily to the three harbours at the base of the cliff, while the island's airport on the east shore enjoys international flights as well as daily Olympic flights from Athens, Mykonos, Crete and Rhodes in summer.

Ascending the 1,000 feet cliff face from the three harbours of Kalderas, Athinos and Oia was not easy in the past. The alternative was a stiff walk or a donkey ride at Calderas and Oia and a wait for a bus or taxi at Athinos in the south.

Calderas, the closest port to Thira, is traditionally reached by a steep zig-zag of 587 stone steps two kilometres long. A ride on a donkey or mule, which most tourists and cruise-ship passengers opted for, could be a hairy business, especially after dark. Many people have ended up riding side-saddle and clutching for dear life to the reins of a rampaging mule with their bags tumbling down the steps or trailing along after becoming dislodged.

However, modern technology has provided an alternative in recent years in the shape of a cable-way carrying 6-person bubbles which whisks visitors up the cliff in two minutes. It was built by an Austrian company at the behest of the Nomikos Foundation of Evangelos Nomikos, which then gifted it to Santorini's 14 communities and ensured the future of the donkey drivers by paying them a small commission from each cable-car ticket.

Rooms can be dear and hard to get in Thira in mid-summer, so arrivals by ships at Oia have a case for getting off there and seeking rooms locally, while those arriving at Athinos should think of taking the first hotel bus that touts for trade or the first rooms they come across, which may be in the village of Messaria at a handy road junction in the middle of the island.

Thira town is undoubtedly the most spectacular place to stay but it can be mean and moody, and a good place to be out of when cruise ships call. Then its narrow pebble-dash streets are crammed with camera-hung trippers, who have only an hour or two to bargain for souvenirs and take photos. The sudden influx turns shopkeepers and donkey-drivers into mercenary maniacs for a short time.

Beaches

Most of the beaches on the island are black sand and pebbles, but nonetheless offer good swimming in warm waters with a slight sulphur smell cheek by jowl with chunks of pumice stone.

Almost the whole of the gently sloping east coast is swimmable. The most popular beaches, with regular buses, are at Kamari, three-quarters of the way down the island, which is turning into a sizeable resort in its own right these days, and Perissa near the tip of the south coast. Both are rich in restaurants and have simple accommodation and watersports, while Kamari also has a campsite and discotheque.

To get away from the crowds, aim halfway down the island at Monolithos, where the sand is a lighter hue, but be prepared for a dusty road around the airport and a not-so-pretty coastline. This is not well served by buses, but as a result attracts fewer people, and it has a cafe with drinks and simple snacks.

There are other deserted coves accessible to scooter and moped riders via the coast road that runs north from Thira to Oia. Akrotiri also has a little beach beneath its archaeological site and it is possible to swim off pebble beaches at all the three ports on the west coast.

If you tire of the popular beaches and find the west coast pebble strips below par, take a boat trip to the nearby islet of Therassia, which has a beach by the harbour and a better one over the hill on the other side of the islet.

Nightlife

Thira has a number of smart bars with smart drinks and smart prices. It also has a variety of scenic restaurants that hang to the cliff. They can be pricey, but worth the money for the unique experience of sipping wine and dining on local fish sitting on a balcony perched 1,000 feet above the sea watching the lights of ships passing below.

The main town also has a clutch of discotheques trading under names like Neptune and Volcan. Kamari also has a disco operating in mid-summer.

Not to be missed on Santorini

Santorini is rich in man-made

antiquities as well as the natural phenomena left behind by the volcanic eruptions. A stunning Minoan city is emerging in the south at Akrotiri, which beats any of those on Crete. There are also Graeco-Roman remains at Ancient Thira, a wine factory which processes the fruit of the island's volcanic soil, the rich monastery of Profitis Elias, and the half-deserted village of Oia in the north which bears witness to the force of the last eruption in the 1950s.

Akrotiri, which can be reached by bus from Thira or Perissa, or by a tour which takes in other wonders of the island, is one of the most important archaeological sites of Greece. There, in a dried-up riverbed, a local farm-worker noticed the tip of an old building 20 years ago and excavations have uncovered a well-preserved Minoan city which has been buried for 3,500 years under lava.

Thanks to the lava, it is in a better state of repair than any of the Minoan cities on Crete and the excavators are making a better job of reconstruction than Sir Arthur Evans did with his imaginative paint job at Knossos. Akrotiri's houses may be under modern corrugated roofs, but they are proper 2-storey houses with recognisable rooms which could be lived in at a pinch.

The tragedy of the site is that the magnificent frescoes of sea battles, African expeditions, children boxing, fashionable women and exotic flowers have been borne away to the Athens Archaeological Museum for safe keeping and fear of volcanic damage. There is talk of them being returned when a strong museum is built on the island, but action would speak louder than words.

If you study the pictures along with

the site, you will soon appreciate that a sophisticated society existed on Santorini from 3000 BC to the big eruption, and may even support my pet theory that the former Atlantis was the centre of Minoan civilisation for a time. The conventional theory is that Santorini was an outpost of Knossos, but it could be turned on its head if a royal palace is unearthed on the island.

Ancient Thira does not set the imagination racing in quite the same way, but is a beautiful little site in a dramatic setting. Mainly Roman, with a market, gymnasium, theatre, baths and Temple of Apollo, it is perched on a shelf above the sea in the south-east of the island with a stunning view towards Anafi.

Profitis Elias is a declining monastery set on the highest peak of Santorini in the lee of a radar station, but its two resident monks are seeing a lively tourist trade these days, thanks to coach tours, and its museum of household items and religious treasures gives an unusual glimpse of religious and island life over the centuries, including a school which flourished underground during the Turkish occupation.

A visit to the half-deserted village of Oia at the northern tip of the island is a must for anyone spending more than a few hours on Santorini because it gives a glimpse of what the villages looked like up to the 1956 earthquake. Some of the old houses are being tastefully restored as guest houses to give an even better impression.

Another pilgrimage worth making is by boat to the two smoking islets in the bay below Thira town, where the volcano still smoulders amidst black cinders. Vegetation is gradually returning, but the scene still resembles something from 'Star Wars'. The only sign of human activity is white paint graffiti plastered over the rocks by the harbour by visiting vandals.

Worth visiting off Santorini

People who have stayed on Santorini for a few days can find the atmosphere a trifle oppressive. It is the feel of an island living next door to a volcano, which sees too many day visitors. However, there are plenty of easy escapes.

The easiest is access to the satellite isle of Therassia, which is delightfully unspoilt beside its parent island. It has rooms and beaches on both sides, so it is a good place for a short stay. Another is by regular ferry to the smaller islands of Anafi, Sikinos and Folegandros.

It is also easy to find a sea connection to Ios, if you want good yellow beaches and don't mind crowds of young people and a booming discotheque scene. Naxos and Amorgos are other good bets by sea, while Olympic Airways offers the chance of flights to Mykonos, Crete and Rhodes.

13. The Blessed Isle – Samos

It is easy to see why the ancients called Samos 'The Isle of the Blessed'. It has an abundance of good things – green, tree-covered hills, orchards, colourful towns, a great range of wines and some of the most spectacular beaches in Greece.

It is the closest of all the big islands to Turkey, separated by only a 3 kilometre strait, and has the most dependable boat connections to that country. It also boasts a good ring road, making all parts of the island easily accessible by bus, car or scooter, and has some of the best outside connections of all Greek islands.

Regular flights from Athens and charter flights from Britain land on the flat coastal strip near Pythagorion, regular ships ply between Samos and Piraeus, calling at one or more of the Cyclades, and the island acts as a junction for shipping routes from the north-east Aegean islands and the Dodecannese. As if that weren't enough, it sometimes has hydrofoil links with Pamos and on to Kos and Rhodes.

The two main ports, and biggest towns on the island, are Samos or Vathi and Karlovassi, both on the north coast. Samos is a lively town with white houses and red roofs, merging into Vathi higher up the hill, but Karlovassi is a dull, sprawling place best visited as a bus halt en route for the great beaches in the west of the island.

Prettier places to stay are Kokkari on the north coast, the old capital of Pythagorion on the south-east coast or in the beach area of Marathokambos in the south-west. Kokkari is a bustling, young resort just 10 minutes from Samos town, while Pythagorion is more up-market with sophisticated restaurants and fancy yachts in its colourful harbour.

All over the island hills and pinewoods give way to terraces of vines and Samos wines are as good as they are varied. They come sweet and brown, dry and pale, resinated yellow, and lusty. Legend has it that the god Bacchus taught the Samians to make wine as a reward for helping him to get rid of the Amazons, who had been rude to him.

Samos was a great power in the ancient world, especially in the 6th century BC when it was ruled by the tyrant Polycrates. He built an empire across neighbouring Aegean islands and ordered the construction of the Temple of Hera, which was ranked as one of the Seven Wonders of the World, and the Efpalinion tunnel to bring water over half a mile to the old capital of Pythagorion.

It was named more recently after the mathematician, Pythagoras, who was a native of Samos in the 6th century BC.

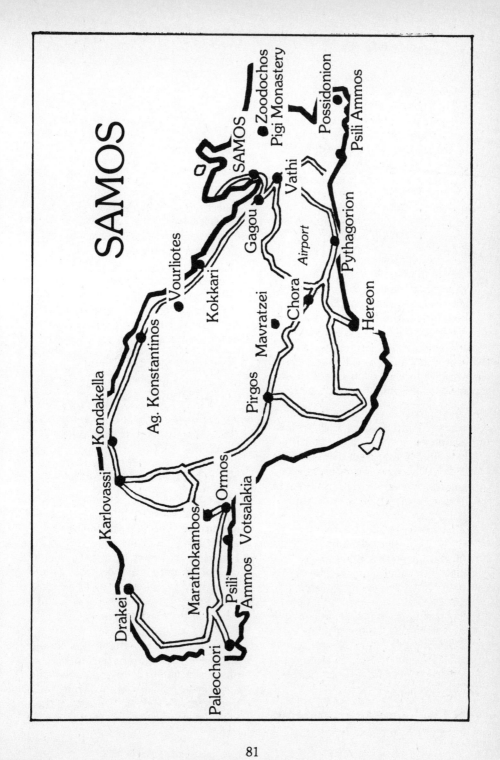

SAMOS

Zoodochos
Pigi Monastery
Possidonion
Psili Ammos
SAMOS
Vathi
Gagou
Pythagorion
Vourliotes
Airport
Kokkari
Hereon
Ag. Konstantinos
Mavratzei
Chora
Pirgos
Kondakella
Karlovassi
Ormos
Marathokambos
Votsalakia
Drakei
Psili
Ammos
Paleochori

Beaches

There are swimmable beaches practically everywhere, but not all are sandy. Samos town has its own shingley beach at Gangou 1 kilometre around the bay, Kokkari has a spectacular big pebble beach with windsurfing and there are pretty shingley coves all the way along the north coast around Kokkari, Agios Konstantinos and Kondakeila. But the best beach on the north coast is in the far north-west beyond Karlovassi at Iamatike Pige, which is a huge crescent of golden sand with a taverna.

The south coast has more sand than the north. There are beaches on both sides of Pythagorion and at Possidonion and Psili Ammos on the south-east shore facing across the straits to Turkey. Both have beach restaurants and are within easy reach by car or bus, or even foot, of both Samos and Pythagorion.

The south-west corner of the island around Marathokambo is almost a continuous strip of sandy bays, the three best-known being Votsalakia, Ormos Marathokambos and Psili Ammos – called like its namesake in the south-east after its 'high sand.'

Nightlife

There is a lively night-time scene along the waterfront of Samos where the tables of every restaurant seem to touch those of another on both sides. Pythagorion also has a great deal of dining out at open-air restaurants by the harbour which are on the expensive side, and Kokkari has a similar scene around the main square. All three places have discotheques and cinemas.

Not to be missed: on Samos

A circular tour of the island is a good idea to take in its beautiful shorescapes, pine-clad hills and monasteries. Pythagorion has the history with the surviving stones and one column of the huge Heraion, or temple of Hera, plus the open jaws of the Efpalion aquaduct, which speak volumes for their 6th century BC builders. There are a few remains of an old theatre nearby.

Both Pythagorion and Samos have museums containing archaeological finds, statues, coins, vases and reliefs from the island's golden age. Samos also has a Byzantine museum.

The oldest monastery on the island, Vrondiani, dating from 1560, is a stiff walk uphill from Kokkari or Agios Konstantinos via Vourliotes, while the Evangelistria is a short walk inland from Votsalakia beach towards Mount Kerkis. The Zoodochos Pigi monastery can be reached by walking up a path from Samos town.

If you like pretty inland hill villages, try Vourliotes, Mavratzei or Pirgos.

Worth visiting: off Samos

There are easy ship connections to Ikaria, and Patmos, but you usually need more than one day to get there and back. Don't miss a day trip to Kusadasi in Turkey from either Samos or Pythagorion, and if possible take in a bus trip to Ephesus, one of the best preserved classical Greek towns in the whole of the Mediterranean.

Visitors staying in Pythagorion should also take a day trip to the gentle offshore island of Samiopoula, which has a pretty beach with taverna, and to the more rocky Agathonissi, if there is a boat going and returning the same day.

14. The Northern Isle – Thassos

Thassos is the most northerly island in Greece, reaching far to the north of Corfu, and boasts a wide variety of scenery, from high mountains and pine forests to broad, gently-sloping beaches of white and yellow sand.

It lies off the shore of northern Greece at the apex of the Aegean Sea. Its greenery, pine trees and olive groves match those of Corfu and Halkidiki, which both lie west of it.

Oil was found off Thassos in the early 1970s and provoked Turkey to lay claim to some of the north Aegean isles and their offshore waters. This explains the presence of Greek soldiers on apparent war footing, dug in on remote beaches, and illuminated platforms out to sea.

It is also one of the most accessible Greek islands, reached in just over an hour by regular, flat-bottomed ferries from Kavala, which is a spectacular provincial town and port with an international airport.

As a result, it is well-populated in summer by campers and motorists with foreign number plates who drive down from Germany, Austria and Yugoslavia and pour across the straits to the island's twin ports, Prinos on the west coast and the capital, Limin or Thassos town on the north.

Yet, Thassos never seems over-crowded. Its coastal ring road, regular bus service, plentiful flatland by the sea and thick forests combine to absorb its many visitors. And you can always hire a bike to escape the crowds.

It is also a welcoming place. The main port greets visitors with a long string of national flags on the dockside and notices in foreign languages covering local hotels and shipping schedules. But it can be noisy in summer when young tourists arrive and the town's discos boom loud and clear into the early hours. Those seeking quiet are better-off staying at Prinos, the second ferry port, or Limenaria, the pretty fishing port in the south of the island, or in one of the many resorts of the east coast.

Beaches

You are never far from a beach on Thassos, but those on the west coast around Prinos are shingley. The best sand beaches stretch round the east coast from Thassos town to Limenaria and many have water-sports such as windsurfing and water-skiing.

Makriammos, a few kilometres walk or bus ride from Thassos town, is the best-known and has good sand, but for most of its long stretch is a pay beach and a trifle too organised for most tastes. Further south, below the spectacular village of Panagia is a good stretch of sand at Chrisi Amoudia ('Golden Bay') and there is another across the bay at Chrisi Akti ('Golden

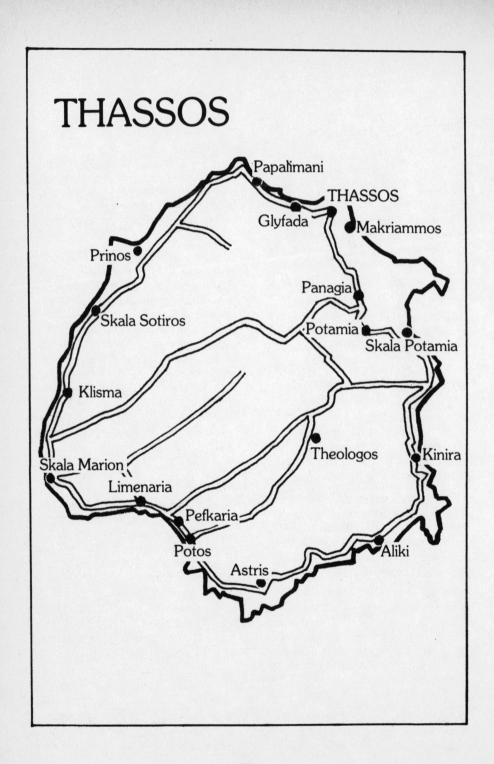

THASSOS

Papalimani

THASSOS

Glyfada

Makriammos

Prinos

Panagia

Skala Sotiros

Potamia

Skala Potamia

Klisma

Theologos

Kinira

Skala Marion

Limenaria

Pefkaria

Potos

Aliki

Astris

shore'). Kinira and Aliki have other good beaches and there are a number of swimmable sandy coves just east of Linenaria around Pefkaria.

Chrisis Ammoudia and Chrisi Akti, or Skala Potamias, as its pretty harbour is called, almost run into one another and offer 2–3 miles of gently-shelving beach with restaurants and small hotels set against a backdrop of plane trees and pine-clad mountains.

Kinira has a small pebble beach and there is another of fine sand a mile or so south opposite Kinira island. Aliki is another pretty harbour village, which has attracted an artists' colony to its slate-roofed houses.

There are other beaches near Potos and Pefkari, including the sandy Psili Ammos, while Limenaria has a long pebble beach.

Skala Marion, south of Prinos on the west coast, has a good sand beach, but the west coast does not compare with the east for scenery.

Nightlife

Nightlife is eating out on the seafront most of the way around the island, but Thassos town has more than its fair quota of discotheques and bars. They rock the waterfront of the port most evenings. An ancient theatre plays host to a festival of classical pieces in the summer.

Not to be missed: on Thassos

Thassos town has the remains of ancient Thassos, including the theatre, Roman agora and three or four temples. You can also trace the old city walls on a pleasant 4-kilometre stroll right around the port, which affords some good views of the island and mainland and passes through a Venetian castle on the hill above the town. The town also boasts a cute little archaeological museum, which seems to specialise in lions, but also has a number of fine statues.

Visitors staying in the main town should make a circular tour of the island to see its pretty bays and villages. It is easy by bus, car or bike, though cyclists need more than a day since the ring road is around 80 kilometres long.

Worth visiting: off Thassos

Regular ferries make it easy to visit the colourful mainland port of Kavala, the Roman remains at nearby Phillipi and even the eastern shores of Halkidiki. There are also ferry connections with the neighbouring islands of Samothraki and Limnos but plan to stay overnight if visiting either since they are about four hours journey.

Limenaria has something of the feel of a German lakeside town, due no doubt to its occupation by a German company at the turn of the century. It is comfortable and has good eating.

Inland Thassos has an abundance of pretty mountain villages, like Panagia, Theologos and Potamia, which have running streams and an Alpine flavour.

15. Shopping and Souvenirs

People don't go to Greek islands for a shopping expedition as they might to London, Paris or the Far East. Yet, they are stacked out with souvenir shops winking with bright colours and only the most insensitive or world-weary will pass them all by.

So long as you keep a completely cool head, inspect a few shops before you make up your mind and then buy only what you really want, you may end up with some treasures and a few bargains.

There is a temptation to buy the first painted heroic plate, icon, or rug for the wall at home because it looks such a beautiful piece of art, until you see the 300th such item and realise they are the height of Greek kitsch and no longer look faintly attractive. Sponges, Greek-pattern shirts and dresses and worry beads all have local appeal too, but will you ever use them at home?

Most of the best buys in Greece are outside the souvenir shops in specialist food, drink, fur, pottery, leather, jewellery, hardware and clothing shops.

You will never go wrong buying olives. Or olive oil, especially the dark green unrefined variety that is sold neat from a barrel. It is the best in the world. So is much of the local fruit, melons, peaches, grapes and the like, though they may not travel well. Greece is one of the great aromatic countries of the world and herbs sold in food shops or supermarkets are worth buying if you can't find your own crop on a scented hillside. So are nuts and Turkish delight.

Local wines are surprisingly cheap and good on big wine-producing islands like Crete, Rhodes, Samos, Kos, Kefalonia and Paros.

If you buy in a shop rather than at the airport, you can almost double your duty-free allowance. Wines from around 200 drachmas are great bargains. This includes retsina which travels and keeps perfectly, just as it was designed to. Brandy, ouzo, liqueurs and gin, from 400 drachmas a bottle are also amazingly inexpensive. Cigarettes are similarly cheap if you can take the harsh taste, which is somehow never so appealing once back in Britain.

Fur rugs and coats, made mainly in the north around Kastoria, are best bought in a fashionable shop, or other sophisticated centres like Rhodes and Mykonos. There you can get a cut to match the skin and not end up looking like an overfed bear.

The same rule goes for pottery, jewellery and leather, although many islands have specialist local potters, who have always made cooking and fancy pots for local consumption.

Greek jewellery, whether silver, gold or simple costume, is up with international standards and rarely overpriced, though that does not mean local shops will drop below the international gold price. In the hardware shops there are some good buys in local lamps, Greek coffee pots and ornamental kebab skewers and, on the islands, the same shops will stock local snorkelling and spear-fishing equipment at much lower prices than Regent Street or Fifth Avenue.

Greek clothing is not always high fashion, but you can find light cotton dresses and patterned headsquares which are ideal for the climate, don't look out of place at summer parties back home and cost less than Woolworth's. Men can usually find denim shorts that fit and are cheap, though they can shrink on their first wash.

Corfu is the Olive isle and olivewood bowls, trays and plates are as good there as anywhere.

It is also a fertile island abounding in food and drink products. It hardly makes sense to bring back yoghurt, but local honey is delicious. So are Loukoumi (Turkish delight elsewhere), nuts, olives and crystallised fruits. Corfiot olive oil has to rank among the best in the world, especially the dark green kind that you can't buy in Western Europe.

Corfu has its own wines and liqueurs, including Koum Kouat, made from tiny Oriental oranges, but try it locally before buying a bottle as it is very, very sweet.

Local sandals, boots and locally-woven cloth are all worth looking out for. Sandals and boots are often made by the shoe-maker on the premises and you can have a pair made to order, especially on big islands like Crete, Paros and Corfu.

Hand-knitted island sweaters are another item worth hunting down. Most of the Cyclades stock them the year round as a natural protection against the driving winds that hit the islands in both mid-summer and mid-winter. They also stock thick fishermen's vests, which have been taken up as high fashion items by many visitors to the Greek islands in recent years.

Mykonos has a whole horseshoe-shaped street of shops selling smart furs, leather jackets and high fashion clothes beside the standard island sweaters and sandals.

Furs never come cheap, but you are likely to get a better bargain in Rhodes than anywhere in Western Europe, thanks to its duty-free status and the hot competition between different shops to drive a bargain. You may also find the fit on the generous side, though, to suit a fuller Greek figure, so don't be in a hurry to buy until you find the cut that is right for you.

The same goes for handbags and high fringed boots, which are a speciality of the village of Archangelos and stand in rows along the village street there. They are sometimes called 'snake boots'.

When it comes to handicrafts you have to look at Rhodian pottery – jugs, bowls, plates, plant pot covers, tiles and drink coasters decorated with fish, flowers, trees, ships and mermaids. In fact, after being on the island for a week or two you certainly will have done because there are pottery factories along the main roads and stalls selling it everywhere including Lindos.

Tour buses regularly make stops at one or more pottery workshops or factories. But it is probably better to buy in town where there is a wider selection and you might be able to bargain more than at the factory.

Much of the pottery is made around Lindos and the same town specialises in lacework table cloths, shawls and table mats. Again you should cast your eye around a good selection rather than jump at one hung outside a house on the main donkey steps winding through Lindos Town.

Rugs are a tricky subject. There are some beauties in skin and wool, notably the flokatis which have featured in Sunday colour mags in recent years. But they can be as dear in Greece as in Britain. The only golden rule is to know what one is worth to you and bargain like crazy for the right price. Or settle for a woven bag.

You can't bargain at the kiosks. Found everywhere, these are a unique Greek invention, open far beyond the usual morning and evening shopping hours, and seem to stock everything you might need urgently, from a ball-point pen to a stamp, a sticking plaster, a telephone, newspaper and sun-glasses.

16. Eating and Drinking

A typical meal in the Greek islands is skewered kebab or souvlakia accompanied by a Greek salad of tomatoes and cucumber topped with feta cheese and black olives. This is true whether you choose to eat in a pistaria (or grill house) or a conventional restaurant.

But in any restaurant in a town or port you will find pre-cooked alternatives like stuffed tomatoes, moussaka, keftedes or meat balls, vegetables in oil and soups. In any restaurant within a mile or two of the sea you are almost certain to be offered fish, most commonly fried squid, grilled marithes or whitebait and barbounia or red mullet.

There is likely to be a sprinkling of Italian dishes too, especially spaghetti and increasingly pizza, reflecting the tastes of the islands' medieval occupants. Chicken and omelettes are also available in most places.

First-time visitors tend to jump at fish when it is offered, and it can be a good choice when it is genuinely fresh and not over-priced, but it pays to check on both points before ordering, remembering that fish kept in a deep freeze for weeks is not fresh and you should not pay £5 a plate when you should be paying £1 or £2. Fish can be the big rip-off of restaurants throughout Greece.

Better to stick to chicken and omelettes, which are always made from fresh ingredients with a natural flavour that you never find in Western Europe rather than be lured into an expensive, disappointing fish dish simply because the sea breeze is blowing and you are watching a marvellous Mediterranean sunset.

The best place to eat fish is where it is a speciality like a harbourside restaurant where the catch comes in each day or a small beach taverna run by a fisherman's family. In the same way, the best and cheapest places to eat souvlakia or kebab are the specialist grill houses or pistarias you find in most big ports.

Greeks usually drink either retsina, the ubiquitous resinated wine, or beer with such meals, but there is often a local wine available on the big islands.

There are also plenty of snacks eaten in other places that make a good supplement to or substitute for a full meal if the weather is hot. Most islands have yoghurt, which is especially delicious with honey. Many of the islands have local honey.

Cheese and olives also make a great snack, whether it is the ubiquitous feta or goat's cheese, graviera or Greek gruyere, or local cheeses like the superb mizithra, a soft white cheese found in central Crete.

Whatever island you are on, try seasonal fruits like strawberries, peaches, apricots, oranges, melon and

ΤΥΡΙΑ	CHEESES		74	ΚΡΑΣΙΑ ΑΣΠΡΑ		WHITE WINES			
Φέτα	Feta			ΡΟΤΟΝΤΑ	1/4	ROTONDA	1/4		
Κασσέρι	Kasseri			ΡΟΤΟΝΤΑ	1/2	ROTONDA	1/2		
Γραβιέρα	Gruyère			ΡΕΤΣΙΝΑ ΜΠΟΥΤΑΡΗ	1/2	RETSINA BOUTARI	1/2		
....	....			ΛΑΚ ΝΤΕ ΡΩΣ	1/4	LAC DES ROCHES	1/4		
....	....			ΛΑΚ ΝΤΕ ΡΩΣ	1/2	LAC DES ROCHES	1/2		
				ΣΑΝΤΟΡΙΝΗ ΜΠΟΥΤΑΡΗ	1/2	SANTORINI BOUTARI	1/2		
ΦΡΟΥΤΑ	FRUITS			ΣΑΤΩ ΜΑΤΣΑ	1/2	CHATEAU MATSA	1/2		
Αχλάδια (κιλό)	Pears (kilogram)			....		....			
Μήλα (κιλό)	Apples (kilogram)		140	....		....			
Πεπόνι	Melon								
Καρπούζι	Watermelon			ΚΡΑΣΙΑ ΡΟΖΕ		ROSÉ WINES			
Κεράσια	Cherries		160	ΡΟΖΕ ΜΠΟΥΤΑΡΗ ΣΕΚ	1/2	ROSÉ BOUTARI SEC	1/2		
Βερύκοκα	Appricots			ΡΟΖΕ ΜΠΟΥΤΑΡΗ ΝΤΕΜΙ ΣΕΚ	1/2	ROSE BOUTARI DEMI SEC	.1/2		
Ροδάκινα	Peaches			_Βερίκεα Σωιλου ιοοος_				160	
Φράουλες	Strawberries			....		....			
....	....			....		....			
....	....			....		....			
ΓΛΥΚΑ - ΠΑΓΩΤΑ	DESSERTS - ICE CREAMS			ΚΡΑΣΙΑ ΚΟΚΚΙΝΑ		RED WINES			
Πάστες	Pastries			ΡΟΤΟΝΤΑ.	1/4	ROTONDA	1/4		
Κανταΐφι	Cadaifi			ΡΟΤΟΝΤΑ	1/2	ROTONDA	1/2		
Μπακλαβάς	Baclavah			ΓΟΥΜΕΝΙΣΣΑ ΜΠΟΥΤΑΡΗ	1/4	GOUMENISSA BOUTARI	1/4		
Παγωτά βανίλια	Ice-Cream Vanilla			ΓΟΥΜΕΝΙΣΣΑ ΜΠΟΥΤΑΡΗ	1/2	GOUMENISSA BOUTARI	1/2		
» σοκολάτα	» Chocolate		160	ΝΑΟΥΣΑ ΜΠΟΥΤΑΡΗ	1/4	NAOUSSA BOUTARI	1/4	320	
» ανάμικτο	» Mixed			ΝΑΟΥΣΑ ΜΠΟΥΤΑΡΗ	1/2	NAOUSSA BOUTARI	1/2		
				ΠΑΡΟΣ ΜΠΟΥΤΑΡΗ	1/2	PAROS BOUTARI	1/2		
				ΚΑΒΑ ΜΠΟΥΤΑΡΗ	1/4	CAVA BOUTARI	1/4		
ΜΠΥΡΕΣ	BEERS		89	ΚΑΒΑ ΜΠΟΥΤΑΡΗ	1/2	CAVA BOUTARI	1/2		
Άμστελ 500 γρ.	Amstel 500 gr.			ΓΚΡΑΝΤ ΡΕΖΕΡΒ ΜΠΟΥΤΑΡΗ	1/2	GRANDE RESERVE BOUTARI	1/2	400	
Χέννινγκερ 500 γρ.	Henninger 500 gr.			ΗΜΙΓΛΥΚΟΣ ΜΠΟΥΤΑΡΗ	1/2	IMIGLYKOS BOUTARI	1/2		
....	....			ΜΑΥΡΟΔΑΦΝΗ ΜΠΟΥΤΑΡΗ	1/2	MAVRODAFNE BOUTARI	1/2		
....	....			....		....			
....	....			....		....			
ΑΝΑΨΥΚΤΙΚΑ	REFRESHEMENTS								
Κόκα-Κόλα	Coca-Cola		60	ΠΟΤΑ		DRINKS			
Λεμονάδα	Lemon Juice		60	ΟΥΖΟ ΜΠΟΥΤΑΡΗ ΜΙΝΙ 55 ΓΡ.		OUZO BOUTARI MINI 55 GR.			
Πορτοκαλάδα	Orange Juice		60	ΟΥΖΟ ΜΠΟΥΤΑΡΗ 155 ΓΡ		OUZO BOUTARI 155 GR.			
Νερό	Mineral water		80	....		....			
Σόδες	Soda		60	....		....			
....	....			ΟΥΙΣΚΥ ΤΕΑCHER'S		WHISKY TEACHER'S			
....	....			CINZANO		CINZANO			
....	....			....		....			
....	....								

| Κουβέρ | Cover Charge | | **5** |
| Άρτος (μερίδα) | Bread (portion) | | 10 |

ΟΡΕΚΤΙΚΑ — **APPETIZERS**

Γαρίδες	Shrimps		329
Καλαμάρια	Squids		398
Χταπόδι	Octapus		
Τζατζίκι	Tzatziki (Garlic Mix)		
Ταραμοσαλάτα	Eggfish Salad		40
Μελιτζανοσαλάτα	Eggplant Salad		70
(handwritten)			80

ΣΟΥΠΕΣ — **SOUPS**

| Κρεατόσουπα | Meatsoup | |
| Ψαρόσουπα | Fishsoup | |

ΖΥΜΑΡΙΚΑ — **PASTA**

| Μακαρόνια | Spaghetti | | 200 |
| Παστίτσιο | Pastizzio | | |

ΨΑΡΙΑ — **FISH**

Αστακός (κιλό)	Lobster (kilogram)		5,000
Μπαρμπούνια (κιλό)	Red Mullet (kilogram)		4,000
Λιθρίνια (κιλό)	Fried Cod Fish (kilog.)		3,500
Μελανούρια	Blacktail		
Μαρίδα	Small fried fish		150
Γαλέος τηγανιτός	Red Snapper		180
(handwritten)			

ΛΑΔΕΡΑ — **COOKED IN OIL**

Μελιτζάνες ιμάμ	Eggplants Imam		200
Φασολάκια φρέσκα	String Beans		250
Μπάμιες *(handwritten)*	Okra		200
Φασόλια γίγαντες	Beans		250
(handwritten)			

ΚΙΜΑΔΕΣ — **MINCED MEAT**

Τομάτες γεμιστές	Tomatoes Stuffed		
Μακαρόνια με κιμά	Spaghetti minced meat		395
Σουτζουκάκια φούρν.	Oven Steaks Piquante		
Μουσακάς	Noussaka		
(handwritten)			395
(handwritten)			395

ΚΥΡΙΑ ΦΑΓΗΤΑ — **MAIN DISHES** — 407

Μοσχάρι: Πατάτες	Veal with: Potatoes	
Γιουβέτσι	Veal in Clay Bowl	
Πιλάφι	Rice	
Μακαρόνια	Spaghetti	407
Αρνάκι: Πατάτες	Lamb with: Potatoes	
Μακαρόνια	Spaghetti	
Πιλάφι	Rice	
(handwritten)		

ΨΗΤΑ — **ROASTED** — 480

Μοσχάρι	Veal	
Αρνί γάλακτος	Lamb	
Γουρουνόπ. σούβλα	Porc Barbecued	
Κοτόπουλο	Chicken	384
(handwritten)	*(handwritten)*	68
(handwritten)		690

ΤΗΣ ΩΡΑΣ — **GRILLED**

Σουβλάκια Μόσχου	Veal on Skewer	
Μπριζόλες Μόσχου	Veal chops	
Χοιρινές Μπριζόλες	Porc chops	550
Μπιφτέκια Σχάρας	Minced Meat Steaks	
Συκώτι Σχάρας	Liver on Grill	
Μπον Φιλέ	Fillet Steak	
Αρνίσια Παϊδάκια	Lamp Chops	

ΣΑΛΑΤΕΣ — **SALADS**

Τομάτα με ελιές	Tomato & Olives	16?
Χωριάτικη	Country Style	334
Μαρούλι	Lettuce	
Λάχανο	Cabbage	566
(handwritten)		

91

grapes. Greece has some of the best fruit in the world and the islands are no exception.

Greek food is loved by some and hated by others. They slate it for its lack of variety, over-use of olive oil, and being served lukewarm. You even hear people say: 'I would go to Greece but for the food. And the wine tastes like disinfectant.'

They have either suffered too much of the bland international package tour food served up by some hotels, or they have not taken the trouble to explore Greek food and wine carefully. An average Greek menu contains a vast variety of dishes and wines. They are pure and healthy, free from cloying preservatives and, like so many of the best things in life, improve on acquaintance.

They suit the climate and convey an unusual sense of luxury for a modest price because in Greece you can eat out in the open air and that much closer to nature, including the fields where the food was raised or the sea where it was caught.

Look at the menu illustrated in this book. It immediately tells you four things. It is in two languages – Greek and English. There is a huge variety of dishes, in a dozen different categories. Most of them are amazingly cheap, even taking the drachma at 250 to the pound for easy reckoning and the second price column, which includes service. And the most expensive items are fish, which are priced per kilo.

Clearly it pays to explore the menu rather than jumping at the first thing offered, which is often fish and is often a rip-off in tourist areas. If there is no written menu, have a look around the kitchen, which is an accepted custom in Greece, or examine the glass-fronted refrigerator in front of the kitchen, which is a standard item in Greek restaurants.

Order there and then, because service can be slow if you are too shy to follow the Mediterranean custom of waving and shouting at the waiter to attract his attention.

Appetizers or starters: These are a mixture of dips like taramosalata (cod's roe), tsajiki (garlic, yoghurt and cucumber) and melitzanasalata (aubergine), soups, which are often more like a stew, and octopus, which is strictly an acquired taste. The first thing to try are the dips, eaten with bread.

Pasta: A legacy of the Italian occupations of Greece, but not usually up to Italian standards.

Fish: Usually good and fresh, but usually expensive too, so tread warily. Greek lobster and shrimps are nothing special and can cost more than the same items in Western Europe without such good dressings. Red mullet is also dear for no good reason, but it is worth trying a small fish or two. Squid and small fish like whitebait, called marithes, are delicious and bargains. Swordfish is usually worth a small premium.

Vegetables cooked in oil: They are delicious when you have acquired the taste, especially beans, but are often served cold and are not the first thing to choose if you are new to Greek food. When you have been in the country a while, though, look out for fried aubergine and marrow.

Pre-prepared meat dishes: These can be delicious when you are used to the way they are cooked early in the day and served lukewarm later. Especially stuffed tomatoes, stuffed aubergines and moussaka.

Grills and A La Minute dishes: This is where people new to Greece should look for their main course, if they want meat because it will be served hot and freshly-cooked. Roast meat, like fish, is often charged by the kilo, but it is not so expensive. Chicken is always good in Greece because it is cheap, and is not reared in a factory and fed on fishmeal. Pork chops and skewered meat are also good buys.

Salads: These are another safe and rewarding area for people new to Greece, whether they fancy a plain tomato salad, plain cucumber or a Greek salad with onions, olives and chunks of cheese added. Don't expect to see lettuce, but try raw cabbage salad if you find it.

Cheese: The main Greek cheese is feta, which is goat cheese. It is rich and creamy, but can be strong for newcomers. There is often an alternative.

Fruits and desserts: Greek fruit is amazingly tasty, especially melon, watermelon, peaches, apricots and grapes, thanks to the climate and its freshness. Apples are the exception that taste better in Britain. Greek ice-cream is also superb, a legacy of the Italians that has lost nothing in the translation.

Drinks: You have probably never read a wine writer praising Greek wines and they are all too often associated with retsina, the golden wine which is laced with pine essence. Personally, I would drink nothing else. It is the cheapest wine in Europe, served in a restaurant for under 50p a 500 centilitre bottle, and a perfect match for Greek food once you get to know it. But there are many other good wines, both local and national, which may better suit a new visitor.

Demestica from Patras comes red and white, is found almost everywhere in Greece and is moderately-priced. The same can be said of other brands like Kamba and Boutari. But be prepared to try local wines, especially on wine-producing islands like Kefalonia.

If you can get along with none of them, try beer, but make sure it is cold. Greek beer tends to be fizzy and chemical compared with English beers. Not a refreshing taste when warm. Greek mineral water is always good.

Ouzo, the aniseed spirit that resembles pernod and turns white in water, may be an acquired taste, but Greek brandy is acceptable to most tastes, so long as it is taken in sparing quantities.

You will not find them on many restaurant menus, but Greek restaurant and bars can turn out superb omelettes. They taste good because the eggs are fresh and they are cooked in olive oil. An omelette and salad with a bottle of wine followed by fresh fruit and coffee can be one of the most satisfying and healthy meals you can eat in the hot noon temperature of Greece.

Coffee is not on many restaurant menus either because it is usually served at separate bars, cafés, pastry shops and coffee houses. In fact drinking coffee is a great ritual in Greece. The standard cup looks like a thimble full of grounds laced with sugar to reduce its bitterness, which is exactly what is is, but is cheap and taken with a glass of water can be lingered over for hours. If you can't take it, ask for 'Nescafee' with milk, which is the standard expression for a big instant coffee.

It often makes sense when dining out

in the evenings to eat a main course, or mixture of savoury dishes, in a restaurant and retire to a pastry parlour or cafe for dessert, coffee and after-dinner drinks. They serve some delicious treacly cakes with eastern names like baclava, Kadifi, galaktaboureko and loukamades, plus yoghurt and honey, chilled rice puddings and custards, but beware of fluffy cream cakes, which are all appearance and taste like cardboard.

It is easy to see that anyone can wine or dine in style in Greece on anything from one simple dish to a 12-course banquet. Either will be good value so long as it is eaten in a typical Greek restaurant.

Unfortunately, their prices bear no resemblance to those of some isolated package tour hotels, which can charge up to two or three times those in the town and turn out worse fare.

17. Helpful Hints

Passports

British visitors to Greece need an up-to-date passport. This can be a regular British Passport (valid 10 years) or a British Visitors' Passport (valid one year only and obtainable from post offices). No visa or vaccination certificates are needed. The same passport regulations apply to nationals from Eire, Australia, USA, Canada, New Zealand and South Africa. You can stay in Greece three months. If you want to work you have to apply for the special residence permit, valid for citizens of the EEC.

Customs

Visitors entering Greece face normal customs regulations on personal belongings and duty-free goods. When leaving Greece, the duty-free allowances for UK residents are as follows:

Cigarettes 300
Cigars 75
Tobacco 400 grams
Spirits 1½ litres
Wine 5 litres
Perfume 75 grams

As for souvenirs, you can take out virtually what you like, **except** for any antiquities or works of art (however small) found in Greece. The penalties for illegal export of antiquities are severe, and permits for export have to be obtained from the Archaeological Service, 13 Polygnotou Street, Athens, or the Ministry of Culture and Sciences.

Time change

Greek Standard Time is two hours ahead of GMT. Greek Summer Time corresponds almost exactly with British Summer Time (March – October) so the two-hour difference applies virtually all year round.

Information

On places, maps, accommodation and festivals

The National Tourist Organization of Greece (NTOG) is the most obvious source of further information. Its worldwide offices will provide leaflets and maps on individual regions, plus lists of all hotels down to C grade. Make use of it, too, for up-to-date information on travel, festivals, museums and special festivities.

Maps

The NTOG have a selection of free good-quality regional maps. Otherwise Edward Stanford Ltd, 12 Long Acre, London WC2 is recommended for more detailed Greek maps.

Books

There are many books that have been written about Greece over the years. Everyone has their own tastes in travel literature, but in London, for a wide selection of books on Greece, we suggest you try the Hellenic Book Service, 122 Charing Cross Road, WC2, Tel: 01-836 7071, Zeno Greek Bookshop, 6 Denmark Street, WC2. Tel: 01-836 2522 and Chapter Travel, 102 St John's Wood Terrace, NW8. Tel: 01-586 9451.

Addresses in Britain

National Tourist Organisation of
Greece,
195 Regent Street,
London W1R 8DL.
Tel: 01-734 5997.

Greek Embassy,
1a Holland Park,
London, W11
Tel: 01-727 8040.

Hellenic Book Service,
122 Charing Cross Road,
London, WC2.
Tel: 01-836 7071.

The Mary Ward Centre & The Mary
Ward Greek Society,
42 Queens Square,
London, WC1.
Tel: 01-831 7711.
Promotes cultural understanding of
Greece through social meetings and
specialist language courses.

Thomson Holidays,
Greater London House,
Hampstead Road,
London NW1 7SD
Tel: 01-387 9321
Leading tour operator in Greece.

Tourist Police

In Greece there's a helpful branch of
the police called Tourist police. They
have the same powers and duties as
regular police, but their special
authority is to help foreigners. Many
have a knowledge of English and can
give all kinds of assistance, ranging
from accident emergencies to just
finding accommodation. It is for the
latter that Tourist police are especially
useful. Their job is to know where
accommodation exists, and in towns
and on the islands they will have lists
of people with rooms to let.

**Remember, wherever you are in
Greece the Tourist police
telephone number is the same – 171.**

Local festivals

Music, drama and wine festivals are
prominent features on the Greek
summer and early autumn calender.
These tend to be large, international
affairs. Almost every island, town and
village hold their own special festivals
throughout the year. These are often
held on the Saints Day of their church,
or in some way relate to local history
or activities such as fishing and wine
making. Find out details of major
festivals from the NTOG or get a copy
of their useful publication, General
Information on Greece.

Money
Currency

Greece has an easy decimal currency
based on the drachma (dr). Bank
notes come in denominations of 1,000,
500, 100 and 50 drachma. There are
also six main coins. The one and two
dr coins are bronze; the 50, 20, 10 and
5 dr coins are nickel.

Where to change money
Banks

Open Monday to Friday 0800–1400.
In main tourist centres some banks
open in the evenings and at weekends
as well.

Banks will change foreign currency
and travellers cheques. Eurocheques
backed by a Eurocard guarantee, can
also be cashed in almost every branch
of the Bank of Greece and other
banks displaying the EC sign. Credit
cards are sometimes accepted. For any
transaction your passport will be
needed.

Hotels and Tavernas

Often even the smallest taverna in
holiday centres will change foreign
currency and travellers cheques.
Usually only the large international
hotels will take personal cheques and
credit cards for payment.

Zakynthos —
The Vasilikos peninsula

Santorini —
A volcanic view

Thassos —
A beach to yourself

FROM ATHENS TO ZAKYNTHOS
THE WIDEST SELECTION OF
HOLIDAYS TO GREECE

For Summer '90 no one offers a better selection of holidays to Greece than Thomson - a selection of 16 islands and 3 mainland areas from a range of 9 brochures. Something to suit all tastes. So whether you're looking for the classical splendours of Athens or the golden beaches of Zakynthos, Thomson has the Greek holiday for you.

There are 9 brochures to choose from offering everything from luxury hotels in "A La Carte" to the freedom of your own holiday home in "Villas & Apartments".

And for those who prefer to sample the truly Greek way of life, none could be better than Thomson Simply Greece - the no. 1 specialist to Greece.

So many islands .... so many holidays.

Let Thomson help you decide

"Where to go in Greece"

Simply **Greece**

Family
C·H·O·I·C·E

VILLAS
AND
APARTMENTS

Small & Friendly

AIR FARES

Young
At Heart

A LA CARTE

Summer Sun

Winter Sun

THE NUMBER ONE
SPECIALIST TO GREECE

Shops

Most shops catering for tourists will accept foreign currency or travellers cheques as payment. The rate of exchange won't be particularly good, though, and any change will be in drachmas.

Travel Agencies

Tickets can usually be paid for in foreign currency or travellers cheques or credit cards.

Tipping

Tipping is much the same as in the UK, but on a more modest scale. On the menus of most restaurants you will notice two prices for each item, the first is without service, the second with service. In most cases the second price is always charged so you only need to leave a few drachmas as tip after your meal.

Health

Full medical insurance is strongly advised for all visitors to Greece. In most cases you have to pay for the treatment at the time of illness/accident and then claim back the money from the insurance company after your return home. Employed people from the UK can get Form E111 from a Social Security Office before leaving Britain. In theory this entitles you to the same medical treatment as Greek citizens, but in practice much of this treatment is not nearly so comprehensive as you would find at home. Most main towns and islands have a hospital where you can obtain emergency treatment (Tel: 166 for information on local medical care). Otherwise, find a local doctor. In towns, cities and major tourist centres, this won't prove a problem, but in quieter rural areas it may be more difficult. In all cases the Tourist police (Tel: 171) should be able to advise you.

Insurance

It is usually cheaper to buy a comprehensive insurance which covers medical expenses, baggage loss or theft. If you do lose any of your personal belongings report it immediately to the police or Tourist police (Tel: 171).

Telephones

The Organismos Telephikinonion Eliathos (known as OTE) run the Greek telephone service. In small towns and villages there are public telephones at most post offices, in large towns the OTE offices are completely separate. Use kiosks, tavernas and shops for local calls. The owners are usually very obliging and will charge the standard rate. Whether at a public telephone, or those at hotels or tavernas, you pay for your call after you have made it, so you don't need a handful of small coins or tokens.

Useful Telephone Numbers

Directory enquiries	131
General information	134
International operator	161
Time	141
Medical care	166
City police	100
Country police	109
Coastguards	108
Tourist police	171
Fire	199
Roadside assistance (24 hours)	104

International Dialling Codes

In principle there is direct dialling from all telephones in Greece to almost anywhere in the world; in practice the system doesn't always work so well, and you need a lot of patience.

Australia	0061
Canada	001
Great Britain/Eire	0044
New Zealand	0064

Telegrams

These can be sent from OTE offices or main post offices.

Post

Opening hours: 0800 – 1300 (APPROX)

Buy your stamps at post offices or from kiosks and shops selling postcards. Post boxes are yellow and can be found in all towns and villages. Parcels and Post Restante letters can be collected from post offices, but remember to take your passport with you.

Shopping

Except in supermarkets and large shops there are definitely no set shopping hours in Greece. The rule to follow is that on the islands and country areas most provision shops open very early, close from approximately 1300 – 1600, and then open again for a few hours in the evening. On Sunday afternoons and Saints Days almost every shop is closed.

Luggage

Even if you go on holiday in the middle of summer, evenings can be cool, especially in the Aegean when the Meltemmi blows. So, take something to cover up bare arms and legs. Open sandals are obviously practical for hot days, but if you want to walk anywhere except roads, pavements or beaches, then something stronger would be advisable. Antidotes to mosquitoes include insect repellant cream, calamine lotion and mosquito plugs and coils. The last are most effective and cheap and can be bought from Greek grocers shops. Medical equipment would wisely include antiseptic cream, a few plasters and the usual aspirin and stomach upset remedies. If you do find the diet of rich oil a little too much, try a glass of two of undiluted lemon juice – it often seems to work. Towels are usually provided in hotels, but bring your own for the beach.

Electricity

220 AC volt electricity is the standard supply, though a few remote area are still on 110 DC volts. Two-pin plugs are widely used in Greece, so it is wise to buy an adaptor for hair dryers, electric shavers, etc.

Travel

Ferries

In a country that's made up of over 1,000 islands, boats are obviously one of the main forms of internal transport. There are about 250 Greek ports in total, all with scheduled ferry connections. To find a comprehensive list of ferry timetables is not often easy, but the NTOG will usually be able to give some advice, or you could buy a copy of the monthly magazine 'Greek Travel Pages' available in the UK from Timsway Holidays, Penn Place, Rickmansworth, Herts, price £5 (inc p&p).

Hydrofoils

A long ferry journey can eat considerably into your holiday time and there are now several fast hydrofoil sevices, cutting sea travel times by anything up to 70 percent. These operate from Piraeus to the Saronic Islands and eastern Peloponnese; and in the Dodecanese from Rhodes to Kos, Patmos and Samos. There's a speed boat service in operation from Patras to Zakinthos and Kephalonia.

Driving

A British driving licence is sufficient – you do not need an international one to drive in Greece.

As in the rest of Europe, drive on the right and overtake on the left are the rules to remember. Otherwise road signs and signals are standard international and can easily be followed. Front seat belts are compulsory and there are now strong 'Drink and Drive' laws.

Taxis
On the islands taxis are an important form of transport and are used for even quite long journeys. Though not as cheap as they were, fares are still low by our standards. In towns fares will be shown on a meter. In country areas you pay by the kilometres, though for longer journeys it is wiser to try and arrange the fare in advance to save any misunderstanding later.

Car Rental
Many British package tours organise special car rental deals for their clients. If you can arrange this, it is usually the cheapest way of hiring a car when on holdiay. Otherwise, there are plenty of car rental firms throughout Greece, including the main holiday islands. The NTOG in London can provide a list of companies but, once in Greece, you will easily be able to find the names of local firms. Rates vary, but renting a car in Greece is not a cheap exercise. Rates quoted hardly ever include the 18 per cent charged for local taxes and collision damage insurance.

Scooters and Motorbikes
Scooters are an ideal way of summer holiday travel. Especially on the islands where the distances aren't great. Most islands and mainlands centres organise scooter hire and the rates are not expensive. On a scooter or motorbike, you can explore small paths and tracks vetoed to cars and often discover the unspoilt and unknown beaches. But, take out a good insurance policy and drive carefully on the unmadeup roads.

Bicycles
Cycling has never really caught on in Greece. The terrain is too mountainous and the summer climate too hot and deters all but the real enthusiast. However, you can usually rent a bicycle cheaply on the developed islands and, if you have your own, ferries hardly ever charge for transporting it.

Language
In Athens, main towns and all but the smallest islands, English (of sorts) is spoken. So, you can really get by on a holiday in Greece without knowing much Greek. However, it is always useful to understand, or recognise, some words and phrases in any language, and we have selected what we consider are the essentials. For anything more specific, buy a good phrase book and/or a dictionary.

SOME USEFUL PHRASES...

How are you?	Ti kanete	Τί κάνετε;
Fine, thank you, and you	Kala, efkaristo, kee sees	Καλά, εὐχαριστῶ, καί σεῖς
What is that?	Ti, eeneh afto	Τί εἶναι αὐτό;
Do you speak English?	Milate Anglika	Μιλᾶτε Ἀγγλικά;
How much is it?	Poso kani afto	Πόσο κάνει; ὑτό
That's too expensive	eeneh poli ahkreeva	Εἶναι πολύ ἀκριβά
I don't understand Greek	Then katalaveno hellinika	Δέν καταλαβαίνω Ἑλληνικά
I want to go to . . .	Thelo na pao sto . . .	Θέλω νά πάω στό ...
Where is . . .	Pou ine	Ποῦ εἶναι
What time is it?	Ti ora ine	Τί ὥρα εἶναι
Can I have . . .?	Boro nah ekko	Μπορῶ νά ἔχω...;

Please give me . . .	Parakalo, dhoste mou	Παρακαλῶ, δῶστε μου
Could you speak more slowly, please?	Boreetah na milate pio siga, parakalo	Μπορεῖτε νά μιλᾶτε πιό σιγά, παρακαλῶ
a single room	ena mono dhomateeo	ἕνα μονό δωμάτιο
a double room	ena diplo dhomateeo	ἕνα διπλό δωμάτιο
with twin beds	meh dio krevatia	μέ δύο κρεββάτια
with balcony, shower	meh balkoni, doos	μέ μπαλκόνι, ντούς
Where are the toilets?	Pou ine i toualettes	Ποῦ εἶναι οἱ τουαλέττες
I'll be staying three days	Tha meeno tris imeres	Θά μείνω τρεῖς ἡμέρες
I am, we are	eemi, eemaste	εἶμαι, εἴμαστε
I have, we have	echo, echoume	ἔχω, ἔχουμε
I don't know yet	Then ksero akoma	Δέν ξέρω ἀκόμα
No, I don't like it	Okhi, then mou aresee	Ὄχι, δέν μοῦ ἀρέσει
Have you any stamps	Echete grahmatosemah	Ἔχετε γραμματόσημα
Walking	meh ta podeea	μέ τά πόδια
Can we camp here?	Boromeh na kataskenosomeh edo	Μπορούμε νά κατασκηνώσουμε ἐδῶ;
Where is the tourist information centre?	Pou eeneh to touristiko grafeeo	Ποῦ εἶναι τό τουριστικό γραφεῖο;
The bill, please	Ton logaryasmo, parakalo	Τόν λογαριασμό, παρακαλῶ
This is not fresh	Afto then ine fresko	Αὐτό δέν εἶναι φρέσκο

SOME USEFUL WORDS . . .

Yes, no	neh, okhi	ναί, ὄχι
Yes (more formal or with emphasis)	malista	μάλιστα
Please, thank you	parakalo, efkaristo	παρακαλῶ, εὐχαριστῶ
Thank you very much	efkaristo polie	εὐχαριστῶ πολύ
Welcome, excuse me, pardon, what, watch out (no exact English meaning)	oriste	ὁρίστε
Good morning, day	kaleemera	καλημέρα
Good evening	kalee spera	καλησπέρα
Good night	kaleenikta	καληνύχτα
Excuse me, I'm sorry	signomi	συγνώμη
Hello	yasou	γειά σου
Goodbye	adio	ἀντίο
The (singular and plural)	o, ee, to	ὁ, ἡ, τό
	ee, ee, ta	οἱ, οἱ, τά
Where, when	pou, pote	ποῦ, πότε
How, who	pos, pios	πῶς, ποιός
Why, because	yiati, dioti	γιατί, διότι
What, nothing	ti, tipota	τί, τίποτα
Good, bad	kalos, kakos	καλός, κακός
Big, small	megalo, mikro	μεγάλος, μικρός
left, right	aristera, dexia	ἀριστερά, δεξιά
cheap, dear	fthino, akrivo.	φθηνός, ἀκριβός
hot, cold	zesto, krio	ζεστός, κρύος
open, closed	anikto, klisto	ἀνοικτός, κλειστός
fast, slow	grigora, sigar	γρήγορα, σιγά
very good	poli kalo	πολύ καλός
new, old	neo, palio	νέος, παλιός
far, near	makria, konta	μακρυά, κοντά

Entrance, exit	issodos, exodos,	εἴσοδος, ἔξοδος
Museum, post office	mousseo, takidromio	μουσεῖο, ταχυδρομεῖο
Hotel, restaurant	xenodokio, estiatorio	ξενοδοχεῖο, ἑστιατόριο
Bank, church	trapeza, ekleesia	τράπεζα, ἐκκλησία
Ruins, toilet	archea, tooaleta	ἀρχαία, τουαλέττα
Bus, stop	leoforio, stasis	λεωφορεῖο, στάσις
Train, station	traino, stathmos	τραῖνο, σταθμός
Danger, take care	kindino, prosekete	κίνδυνος, προσέκετε
Upper, lower	ano, kato	ἄνω, κάτω
Beach, sea	paralia, thalassa	παραλία, θάλασσα
Aeroplane, airport	aeroplano, aeroporto	ἀεροπλάνο, ἀεροδρόμιο
Ship, small boat	vapori, varka	βαπόρι, βάρκα
At, in (side)	sto, mesa	στό, μέσα
To, from	pros, ahpo	πρός, ἀπό
After, before	meta, prin	μετά, πρίν
And, or	ki, ee	καί, ἤ
Here, there	edo, eki	ἐδῶ, ἐκεῖ
Now, then	tora, tote	τώρα, τότε
With, without	meh, horis	μέ, χωρίς
One, two	ena, dio	ἕνα, δύο
Three, four	tria, tessera	τρία, τέσσερα
Five, six	pende, exi	πέντε, ἕξι
Seven, eight	efta, okto	ἑφτά, ὀκτώ
Nine, ten	ennea, deka	ἐννέα, δέκα
Twenty, fifty	ikosi, peninda	εἴκοσι, πενήντα
Hundred, thousand	ekato, hilia	ἑκατό, χίλια
Sunday, Monday	kiriaki, deftera	Κυριακή, Δευτέρα
Tuesday, Wednesday	triti, tetarti	Τρίτη, Τετάρτη
Thursday, Friday	pempti, paraskevi	Πέμπτη, Παρασκευή
Saturday, today	Savato, simera	Σάββατο, σήμερα
Month, week	mina, evdomada	μήνα, ἑβδομάδα
Morning, evening	proi, vradi	πρωΐ, βράδυ
food and drink	fayita kee pota	φαγητό καί ποτά
table, menu	trapezi, katalogos	τραπέζι, κατάλογος
glass, bottle	potiri, bukali	ποτήρι, μπουκάλι
beer, wine	bira, krassi	μπύρα, κρασί
salt, pepper	alahti, piperi	ἁλάτι, πιπέρι
oil, lemon	lahdi, lemoni	λάδι, λεμόνι
bread, butter	psomi, vutiro	ψωμί, βούτυρο
coffee, tea	kafes, tsai	καφές, τσάϊ
jam, honey	marmelada, meli	μαρμελάδα, μέλι
eggs, fried	avga, tiganita	αὐγά, τηγανητά
milk, sugar	gala, zahkaree	γάλα, ζάχαρη
water, lemonade	nero, lemonada	νερό, λεμονάδα
ice cream, yoghurt	pahgoto, yaouriti	παγωτό, γιαούρτι
soup, fish	soupa, psari	σούπα, ψάρι
mullet, lobster	barbouni, astakos	μπαρμπούνι, ἀστακός
meat, cheese	kreas, tiri	κρέας, τυρί
beef, veal	vodino, moskari	βοδινό, μοσχάρι
pork, chicken	hirino, kotopoulo	χοιρινό, κοτόπουλο
lamb, suckling pig	arnaki, gurunopoulo	ἀρνάκι, γουρουνόπουλο
ham, sausage	zambon, loukaniko	ζαμπόν, λουκάνικο
salad, tomatoes	salata, tomates	σαλάτα, ντομάτες
potatoes, beans	patates, fasolia	πατάτες, φασολ

omelet	omehletah	ὀμελέττα
fruit, apples	fruita, milia	φρούτα, μῆλα
grapes, melon	stafilia, peponi	σταφύλια, πεπόνι
resinated wine, ouzo	retsina, uzo	ρετσίνα, οὖζο

18. Weather in a land of all seasons

If you are planning a trip to Greece in July or August, especially late July or early August, take plenty of sun cream, a tube of insect repellant and a hat. If you go without booking, a light sleeping bag might be a useful optional extra especially on major tourist islands. This is high season, and it can be both uncomfortably hot and crowded these days. August has an additional hazard. The meltemmi wind blows hardest across the Aegean during the month and, though it can cool the nights marvellously, it can also make swimming and lying on a beach a lot less pleasant.

The heat beckons alluringly to refugees from an English summer, but it is too easy to forget that most of Greece is on a level with North Africa. So, don't throw yourself upon Apollo's altar as a burnt sacrifice, especially if the meltemmi is blowing hard and disguising the full blast of the furnace. The temperature is probably around 92 degrees in the sheltered shade. You can feel it well enough later that night when you lie turning on the spit in bed.

The Greek Tourist Office are now curbing their straightforward promotion efforts because they are worried that there are not enough beds for visitors in July and August. Hence their recent campaign to spread tourists through the year by advertising the undisputed charms of the Greek spring and autumn, and across the areas of the country that are not so popular. Witness the money and promotion devoted to Halkidiki. Both campaigns have great intrinsic merit, but if you have to go in July or August because of school holidays, try to make it early July or late August and be prepared for a few problems with accommodation if you haven't already booked any. Hence my suggestion of carrying a light sleeping bag for spending a night on a beach or the deck of a ship between islands.

The best months of the year, to combine heat and perfect weather with a civilised choice of accommodation and more of the true Greek atmosphere are June and September. June is less crowded and the countryside is a blaze of flowers, but the sea is warmer in September. June has the first flush of hot weather fruit – strawberries, peaches and apricots. September has the grape season, figs and succulent melons.

May and October come close on all these counts, especially late May and early October. The weather is usually warm, particularly in the south Aegean; everywhere is less crowded; prices tend to fall or be negotiable. May has an abundance of flowers and the feel of a hot English summer. The sea stays warm through October.

November, December, March and April are ideal for people who want to

103

flee the tourists, but still see the sites. They resemble good English spring or September weather. You can swim without discomfort in a swimming pool and even in the sea around mid-day through November and December. March and April have the added bonus of the Greek Easter festivals, when every church sparkles with flowers and music, and the awakening countryside mirrors the celebrations, with nature bursting into bloom everywhere.

The winter months of November to April are less warm, but still sunny and delightfully uncrowded. In January and February Greece experiences something of a winter with snow falling on the mountains in the north, and Mount Parnassus becomes one of the sunniest ski resorts in Europe. Last year there were still traces of snow in the mountains as late as May.

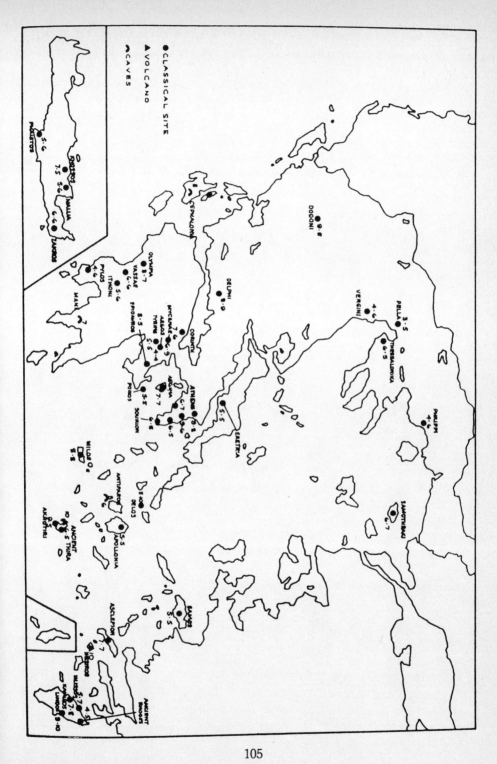

- CLASSICAL SITE
▲ VOLCANO
▲ CAVES

PHAISTOS 5·6
KNOSSOS 7·5 MALLIA 5·6
GOURNIA 6·6

CEPHALONIA

DODONI 8·9

PYLOS 4·6
ITHOMI
OLYMPIA 8·7
VASSAE 6·6
MANI
EPIDAUROS 8·5
MYCENAE 7·6 DELPHI 8·9
ARGOS 8·5
TIRYNS 8·4
CORINTH

VERGINI
PELLA 3·5
THESSALONIKA 6·5

PHILIPPI 4·6

POROS
AEGINA 7·7
ATHENS 8·8
SOUNION 8·5 6·5 8·6
ERETRIA 5·5

MILOS 8·8

ANTIPAROS 8·6
DELOS

ALIGOTHOI 9·5
ANCIENT 10 9·5 THIRA
APOLLONIA 5·5

SAMOTHRAKI 6·7

SAMOS 5·5

ASCLEPION 8·7

HERAION

MILETOS 5·7
KAMIROS 7·8
LINDOS 9·10
ANCIENT KNIDOS 4·5

105

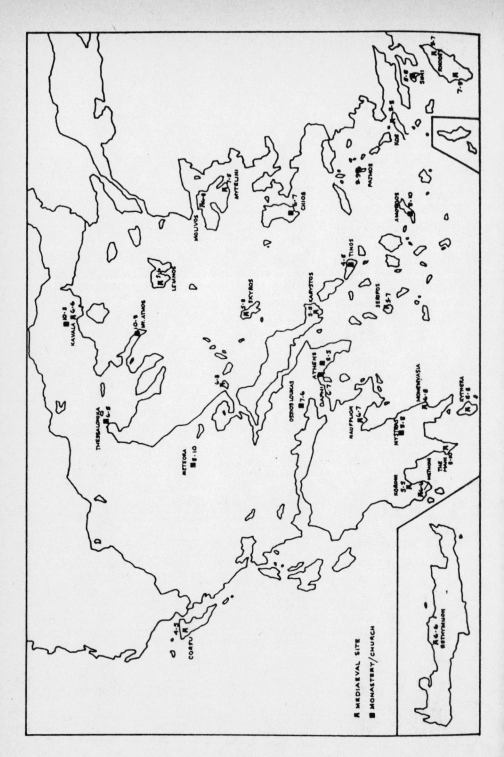

R MEDIAEVAL SITE
■ MONASTERY/CHURCH

TOP TRAVEL TITLES FROM SETTLE PRESS

The following books by Trevor Webster all feature in the highly popular series WHERE TO GO IN GREECE published in association with Thomson Holidays.

WHERE TO GO IN GREECE
by Trevor Webster
An up-to-date, easy-to-read, illustrated guide to the islands and mainland centres, containing a wide range of travellers' advice based on the author's recent personal impressions.

£5.99 paper 0907070264 ☐
3rd reprint 1986
(Revised Edition)

"If only I'd had Trevor Webster's Where To Go in Greece . . . ! Annette Brown **Daily Star**

"an exceptional title for both those seeking culture and the sun". **The Bookseller**

CORFU AND THE IONIAN ISLANDS
by Trevor Webster
Travellers are offered a modern Garden of Eden with Trevor Webster as their personal guide.

£9.99 hard 0907070329 ☐
£6.99 paper 0907070272 ☐
featuring 32 pages of full
colour: publication
November 1986

RHODES AND THE DODECANESE ISLANDS
by Trevor Webster
The appeal and atmosphere of Rhodes and the nearby islands, including tiny Kassos and Symi with its stunning harbour are brought to life by Trevor Webster

£9.99 hard 0907070353 ☐
£6.99 paper 0907070310 ☐
featuring 32 pages of full
colour: publication
April 1987

ATHENS, MAINLAND AND THE NORTH AEGEAN ISLANDS
by Trevor Webster

£9.99 hard 0907070337 ☐
£6.99 paper 090707280 ☐
Featuring 32 pages of colour
Publication November 1986
Publication November 1986

Athens within an hour or so of beach resorts is a perfect staging post for visiting the spectacular sites of Peloponnese, Delphi and Cape Sounion and for the ferries to the islands. Trevor Webster takes the reader on a magic tour of the mainland and over twenty islands.

CRETE AND THE CYCLADES ISLANDS
by Trevor Webster
Crete and the Cyclades are islands of great colour, character and contrast. The atmosphere of their stupendous mountains, beaches, harbours, folklore and history is relayed by Trevor Webster.

£9.99 hard 0907070388 ☐
£6.99 paper 090707396 ☐
Publication November 1987

WHERE TO GO IN SPAIN
A guide to the Iberian peninsula
by H. Dennis-Jones

£9.99 hard 0907070426 ☐
£5.99 paper 0907070434 ☐

Adding to the wide canvas of the Settle Press travel series, it contains rating guides for all the Spanish coastal regions and colourful descriptions of the interior.

NOTES